Begin experiencing t... wonderfully well-wri..., page by page journey to becoming all God intends.

**RICH CARNEY**
Chief Operating Officer, Vision360, Orlando, Florida

Joe creatively connects the dots, aligns theology with real-life application, and shares stories as only a true communicator can. This book is more than a read; it is a journey to embracing the blessing of being human, unique, and a follower of Christ. Joe challenges without compromise, but in a way that is graceful and truly a blessing. You will be touched and changed by this book.

**DRIES LOMBAARD**
Founder and owner, Africanmosaic and Talentmosaic, South Africa

*The Language of Blessing* will lead to new self-understanding that is a solid starting place for a disciple of Jesus who is on the road to becoming more like him. After you journey through this process of becoming more self-aware, you can't help but grow into a better person.

**JAMES J. PUCHY**
Chaplain (colonel) US Army, retired; managing director, national and strategic ministries, American Bible Society

With his rich experience in strengths-based leadership as well as personal and spiritual formation, Joe artfully weaves together stories from his own journey and poignant insights from others to teach us the language of blessing—one he has learned, at times painfully, in the school of life.

**DR. SAM RIMA**
Author, *Overcoming the Dark Side of Leadership*; executive pastor, Tenth Church, Vancouver, British Columbia

Joe Cavanaugh has done a wonderful job of weaving in the concept of blessing and our own uniqueness into a format that lends itself to action. What an engaging book!

**JOSEPH VALENTINE DWORAK**
Director of Admissions, College of Adult and Professional Studies, Graduate School, and Seminary, Bethel University, St. Paul, Minnesota

As you'll discover in *The Language of Blessing*, Joe is encouraging, insightful, and passionate about helping people find their God-given strengths and unique calling. His ideas are just as relevant to any business or other organization as they have been to our church.

**ANDY ROLLER**
Executive pastor, Northwood Church, Keller, Texas

Joe teaches us how to make positive language a natural part of our daily conversations. His application exercises are simple and easy to apply. Every Christian and every parent will appreciate this book.

**JOHN NORRIS**
Director of pastoral ministry, Archdiocese of San Francisco

Drawing from personal experiences, Joe weaves together the biblical principle of blessing with important sociological research to teach us how to "speak" the language of self-awareness and mutual affirmation.

**LARRY S. DOYLE**
Director of Missions for the Piedmont Baptist Association, Greensboro, North Carolina

*The Language of Blessing* is written for immediate application and life-changing impact. Joe's book will enlighten and encourage you, and it will give you practical steps and tools to walk in the power of blessing.

KATIE DRIVER
Trainer and Coach at CMA Resources and House2House Ministries

I highly recommend *The Language of Blessing* to all who want to speak into the lives of others with gracious impact.

JOSEPH H. HOLLOWAY
Lead Pastor, Valley View Church of the Nazarene
Life Coach and Discipleship Trainer

*The Language of Blessing* offers a deeply profound look at who we are and how we have been uniquely created. I believe this book will touch many deeply.

STEPHANIE MOORE
Cofounder, Catholic Strengths and Engagement Community

Joseph helps you awaken to what you've been blind to— your precious interior gifts. Knowing and expressing these gifts will help you deepen your spirituality and offer more meaning to the lives of others.

RYAN M. NIEMIEC
Education Director, VIA Institute on Character; author of *Mindfulness and Character Strengths*; coauthor of *Positive Psychology at the Movies*

Joseph Cavanaugh helps us decipher the God-designed "spiritual code" embedded in every human soul—the gifts that make each one of us one in a trillion. *The Language of Blessing* is itself a blessing, visionary yet intimate, bold and humble.

MARK HERRINGSHAW
North American director, Youth with a Mission Associates

I was deeply moved by the message of love, hope, and grace expressed in Joe's book. He reminds us of the power of our words to build or destroy, as well as the amazing opportunities we have to inspire others to be all they were designed to be.

**MIKE AND TESSA DODGE**
Strengths Network—South Pacific

Five stars for wise insight, clear writing, and solid help.

**DR. DAVID FRISBIE**
Executive director, The Center for Marriage & Family Studies, Del Mar, California

*The Language of Blessing* will not only bless you, but it will provide you with the insight to bless others!

**BOB TIEDE**
Director of global operations leadership development, Campus Crusade for Christ (CRU)

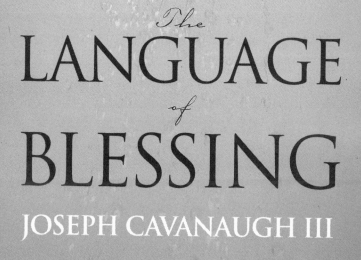

*The*
# LANGUAGE
*of*
# BLESSING

## JOSEPH CAVANAUGH III

TYNDALE
**MOMENTUM**

*An Imprint of Tyndale House Publishers, Inc.*

**BARNA**

Visit Tyndale online at www.tyndale.com.

Visit Tyndale Momentum online at www.tyndalemomentum.com.

*TYNDALE* is a registered trademark of Tyndale House Publishers, Inc. *Tyndale Momentum* and the Tyndale Momentum logo are trademarks of Tyndale House Publishers, Inc. *Barna* and the Barna logo are trademarks of George Barna. Tyndale Momentum and BarnaBooks are imprints of Tyndale House Publishers, Inc.

*The Language of Blessing: Discover Your Own Gifts and Talents . . . Learn How to Pour Them Out to Bless Others*

Designed by Julie Chen

Published in association with the literary agency of Esther Fedorkevich, Fedd and Company Inc., 606 Flamingo Drive, Austin, TX 78734.

To protect the privacy of those who have shared their stories with the author, some names and details have been changed.

Unless otherwise indicated, all Scripture quotations are taken from the *Holy Bible*, New Living Translation, copyright © 1996, 2004, 2007 by Tyndale House Foundation. Used by permission of Tyndale House Publishers, Inc., Carol Stream, Illinois 60188. All rights reserved.

Scripture quotations marked NIV are taken from the Holy Bible, *New International Version,*® *NIV.*® Copyright © 1973, 1978, 1984, 2011 by Biblica, Inc.™ Used by permission of Zondervan. All rights reserved worldwide. www.zondervan.com.

Scripture quotations marked TLB are taken from *The Living Bible*, copyright © 1971 by Tyndale House Foundation. Used by permission of Tyndale House Publishers, Inc., Carol Stream, Illinois 60188. All rights reserved.

Scripture quotations marked AMP are taken from the *Amplified Bible,*® copyright © 1954, 1958, 1962, 1964, 1965, 1987 by The Lockman Foundation. Used by permission.

Scripture quotations marked NASB are taken from the New American Standard Bible,® copyright © 1960, 1962, 1963, 1968, 1971, 1972, 1973, 1975, 1977, 1995 by The Lockman Foundation. Used by permission.

**Library of Congress Cataloging-in-Publication Data**

Cavanaugh, Joseph.
  The language of blessing : discover your own gifts and talents— learn how to pour them out to bless others / Joseph Cavanaugh.
    p. cm.
  Includes bibliographical references.
  ISBN 978-1-4143-6393-6 (pbk.)
 1. Self esteem—Religious aspects—Christianity. 2. Self perception—Religious aspects—Christianity. 3. Interpersonal relations—Religious aspects—Christianity. 4. Parenting—Religious aspects—Christianity. 5. Blessing and cursing. 6. Affirmations. I. Title.
  BV4598.24.C38 2013
  248.4—dc23                                              2012042071

Printed in the United States of America

| 19 | 18 | 17 | 16 | 15 | 14 | 13 |
|----|----|----|----|----|----|----|
| 7  | 6  | 5  | 4  | 3  | 2  | 1  |

# *Dedication*

To my Grandma Sadie, Grandma Grace, Grandpa Mike, Uncle Merle, and Aunt Helen. In my family, they were my advocates, the ones who consistently blessed me with their kindness, words of encouragement, and warm affection. They were my oasis, the refuge of my youth.

To my grandchildren, Hannah, Connor, and those children yet to come (including one expected by the time this book comes out). They have inspired me to be a source of blessing in their lives and are truly one of the greatest joys life has to offer.

To my five sons, Joseph, Christopher, Jonathan, Michael, and Jeffrey, who had to endure my journey of growth and self-awareness. To my dear wife, Jaynee, who has not only endured my journey with near saintly patience but has always been a wonderful mother to our sons.

To William Crum, Charles Schmitt, and Gerry Cheney. When I was a younger man, these men encouraged me to believe that God had called me to a special future.

And finally to Dr. Donald O. Clifton, who revolutionized our understanding of our unique potential and design. I had the opportunity to meet him only once, but his passion and enthusiasm for each person's uniqueness left an indelible impression, which I carry with me to this day.

# Contents

# *Foreword*

Joe Cavanaugh is an interesting guy. As you'll discover in the pages of this book, he has had a variety of fascinating experiences in life.

I first met him in Germany a few years ago at a conference where we were both speaking. He was working with Gallup at the time, helping organizations (including numerous churches and parachurch entities) use Gallup's StrengthsFinder self-assessment, a heavily researched diagnostic tool designed to help users recognize their strongest talents. Through his work with that resource, he was able to engage in a lot of executive coaching related to the insights generated from that strengths inventory. As we got to know each other, I found him to be a kindred spirit and a man with a fertile and curious mind. Such people are usually energetic, fun, and stimulating, and Joe was no exception.

In *The Language of Blessing,* Joe shares with you some of the insights that he has developed over the years through a combination of scientific research, personal experience, biblical education, and professional development. Joe will also introduce you to some self-assessment inventories, which will enable you to invest yourself more heavily in using your strengths rather than inefficiently striving to overcome your weaknesses.

With his intimate knowledge of these inventories, Joe will encourage you to embrace and capitalize upon your uniqueness, talents, and potential. The more you become aware of those special qualities, the more you will be capable of accepting blessings and giving them to others.

At the core of Joe's perspective is the notion that life is all about relationships: with God, the church, family, friends, and all the others we encounter in our daily excursions. The critical aspect of those relationships is not simply having them; it's how we cultivate them that matters.

With that challenge in mind, prepare to reconsider your understanding of the concept and practice of blessing. God has intentionally and lovingly blessed us in many ways. Other people have blessed you throughout your life as well. What is your obligation with those blessings? Do you know how to recognize and receive them? How to share a blessing with others? How to express gratitude for blessings? Joe will not only challenge you with such questions; he will guide your thinking about these issues and help you respond in ways that are consistent with God's plan for your life.

In fact, receiving and giving the blessing is a skill that needs to be developed and refined, just like any other skill. And that's why Joe has written this book: to aid you in the development of the abilities, character traits, and perspectives that will enable you to be blessed and to bless others. This is the essence of life. After all, God underscored to Abraham that we are blessed so that we can be a blessing—to Him and to others (Genesis 12:1-3).

You are unique and talented. That's a truth that deserves to be celebrated—and shared. *The Language of Blessing* will help you do it.

George Barna
Ventura, California
October 2012

# Introduction

Do you realize that you are unique? Do you understand that you are unrepeatable, that there has never been anyone like you before and there will never be again? Do you know that you have been given a unique gift to offer to the world?

As a leadership coach, I often ask clients these very questions. If you are like most of them, your answer is probably, "Uh, no, that is not how I think of myself." Most people do not believe they are "gifted" or possess the stuff of genius. Most people see themselves as pretty average, and this assessment forms the foundation of their self-identity.

I want to convince you that what you offer is so rare that it has never been given before and it will never be given again. Your gift is meant to be used for the benefit of others—and to give you great joy whenever you use it to help someone else.

While your gift is unique, the fact that you are so distinctly blessed is not. Everyone you know has a unique gift to share as well. Your mom and dad, your brother or sister, your spouse, your children—even that whiny neighbor or annoying coworker—each has been given a wonderful gift intended to be used to make our world a better place. And the way each of us sees the world and processes our gifts—what I call our unique genius—is distinctive. Research, however, shows that most people consistently downplay their talents, gifts, and accomplishments. I have observed this tendency as well. Most of us, I believe, have been conditioned to minimize who we really are.

That's certainly what was modeled to me. Then, when my wife and I had our own sons, I discovered something fascinating. When they were very young, we rejoiced over every little step of progress—their first words, their first steps, their first few tentative pedals on the bike, their first hit in Pee Wee baseball. We encouraged any emerging talent we spotted in the classroom, on the ball field, and elsewhere.

As our sons got a bit older, my expectations began to grow, and I became more critical and less encouraging about my sons' activities. Eventually, my words of affirmation became rarer, and my speech became an almost constant stream of criticism. How horribly sad.

That's not the kind of father I wanted to be. Yet I found that affirming my sons was far more complicated than I had imagined. After all, I was discovering that my boys are very different from me. Some of those differences were challenging, hard to understand, and sometimes even difficult to see as positive traits.

I had heard innumerable times how blessed we are as Christians, yet I was struggling to bless others, especially my five sons and my wife. I was also very concerned about the inexplicable bouts of anger I felt over seemingly minor things, particularly any form of criticism directed at me. The words bursting from my mouth in those moments of anger were anything but a blessing to those on the receiving end. Something was very wrong; something felt broken inside of me, and I needed to address it immediately.

I took a major step forward in 1989 when I started a small ministry called New Life, a Christ-centered, twelve-step program for people in relational crisis. Even though I had been a Christian for seventeen years by that point, I did not yet understand or know what God meant when He called us to bless others. During the next ten years at New Life, seven thousand people participated in a journey to a new relationship with God that led to healing, self-discovery, and blessing. What I learned in partnership with those involved in New Life has informed my work since then, including this book. More important, it changed the way I related to those closest to me, especially my wife and my sons.

Just a few years before New Life Ministries was launched, Gary Smalley and John Trent released the bestselling book *The Blessing*. Drawing on their work as family counselors, Smalley and Trent introduced readers to the biblical concept of the blessing and explained why it is so critical that children receive the blessing from their parents. They define the blessing as having five components: touching in a meaning-ful and appropriate way, speaking affirming words, attaching high value to the child, picturing a special future for him or her, and actively committing to help the young person fulfill the blessing.[1]

Smalley and Trent's book remains an invaluable resource, and I did not set out to rewrite it. *The Language of Blessing* developed as a result of my own experiences as a ministry facilitator and life coach. I found that people often struggle to speak meaningful words of affirmation that communicate their child's value and specifically confirm his or her unique design.

This book differs from *The Blessing* in several ways. First, while working with New Life, I uncovered a number of common tendencies that prevent many parents from affirm-ing their children and envisioning their future. Simply put, our differences sometimes lead to tensions, misunderstand-ings, and even broken relationships. For this reason, the book examines some well-intended behaviors that become gift, talent, and character blockers, which I call the Cycle of False Identity. I wrote this book to help you recognize this destructive pattern, which tends to perpetuate itself from generation to generation—as it did in my own family.

If you are often disappointed in yourself or frustrated with other people, this book will help you better under-stand the source of your discouragement and give you some practical tools to move beyond it.

Second, although I learned a lot about family systems

at New Life, my work over the past decade has been as a leadership and strengths coach rather than a family counselor. That means I'm particularly interested in helping people—whether parents, lay leaders, or supervisors—draw out the best in those they lead and influence. No two people think, relate, learn, or are motivated in exactly the same way, and as people discover the unique design God put inside them, many come alive in a totally new way. On top of that, they are in a better position to affirm the special giftedness in others.

Finally, scientific breakthroughs over the past twenty-five years have offered new insights into the importance of the blessing, as well as hope that those who never received it from their parents can still experience it later in life. At the same time, sociological research has demonstrated why our culture's focus on self-esteem and individualism, which are intended to make people feel better about themselves, is such a poor substitute for the blessing.

This book will help you gain a deeper understanding of your own mix of personality, gifts, talents, and character. Through this journey of discovery, you will begin to see how dramatically different your gifts and talents are from the gifts and talents of those you most care about. These differences can create a rich diversity within families and communities. You'll also discover how to affirm others by beginning to uncover the abilities that they, as unique creations of God, possess in surprising abundance and variety. The process of recognizing, encouraging, and affirming one another's unique gifts can become one of life's most joy-filled experiences.

I wrote *The Language of Blessing* with an emphasis on application rather than just theory. For that reason, each chapter ends with questions or examples to help you put the principles into practice.

And so your journey of discovery begins.

*Part 1*

# WHAT IS THE LANGUAGE OF BLESSING?

*Chapter 1*

# THE BLESSING

As a child, I loved visiting my maternal grandmother on her farm in western Iowa. Grandma's yard was bursting with vibrant flowers from early spring to late fall. She knew just how to cultivate a scene blooming with every color of the rainbow for each season. As a young child, I thought every yard should look that way.

However, the view from the house where I grew up was nothing like Grandma's. Our poor yard was a rather forlorn and neglected affair. My father didn't seem to care about it, other than occasionally dragging out a hose and sprinkler when our sparse grass began to turn brown in the summer's heat.

Two huge silver maple trees, one in our front yard and

one in the back, provided a bit of shade. The only other plants were white spirea (bridal wreath) bushes, which grew along the front of our house. Every home on both sides of our block seemed to have those same bushes growing in the front yard. The spirea would bloom in May for a couple of weeks, and the arching cascades of pure white flowers with their golden centers did look beautiful. But then all too soon, the display would be over until the next May.

As if our yard were not plain enough, there was an ugly scar in the front of our lawn. The rut had been worn by the neighborhood kids and my siblings as they took a shortcut from the sidewalk to the walk that led up to our house. I am sure I sometimes took the same shortcut when I was in a hurry.

But by the time I was ten, I saw that ugly rut as an insult to our yard and our home, and I decided to take on a landscaping project. I wanted to do something about that rut and at the same time bring color and beauty to our home. My plan was to plant a closely spaced row of beautiful hybrid tea roses along our front walk. No one would think about cutting through the rosebushes, which have sharp, one-inch-long thorns! As this vision of landscaping glory began to take form in my imagination, I could see this row of roses becoming the envy of the neighborhood.

I had learned from Grandma that I'd have to choose a hardy rose that would thrive in our climate. I did my research by reading a book on roses at our local plant nursery. One picture of a particular rose jumped out at me—the

Peace rose. As the Peace rosebuds begin to bloom, they are a bright yellow, but when they are fully opened, the color mutes to a pinkish cream with a radiant yellow center. The rose is so beautiful that the Germans named it Gloria Dei, or "glory to God." In America, it was named the Peace rose, since Field Marshal Alan Brooke had refused the honor of having it named after him following the end of World War II. He said he would prefer Peace, a name that would be remembered far longer than his, and the name stuck. Since my dad served in WWII, I thought he would find that information fascinating.

As it turned out, potted Peace roses were too expensive for my limited budget. Fortunately, the helpful people at Earl May Nursery told me I could get a bare root plant that would be much cheaper. When I explained I did not yet have all the money, they were kind enough to hold five plants for me. They also explained that I would need peat moss, compost, mulch, and rose fertilizer. This was going to be much more expensive than I had hoped.

I dedicated the next month to doing any kind of odd job I could find in our neighborhood, like digging dandelions, mowing and raking yards, hauling trash, and clearing out brush. Once I had earned enough money to purchase one of the items, I would ride my bike the two miles to the nursery and then bring the purchase back to the house, where I'd hide it under our front porch.

Finally, the day came when I was able to buy the rosebushes. The next day would be D-day . . . digging day.

I rushed home from school that afternoon so I would have time to finish the project before my dad got home from work. I dragged everything I would need out from under the front porch. Using my twelve-inch wooden ruler from school, I began to carefully measure out two feet from the front walk and two feet between the rose plants.

I would be planting the bushes a bit closer than recommended, but I wanted the roses to be an effective deterrent to anyone taking a shortcut through the lawn. All this activity began to draw a small crowd of neighborhood kids, much to my exasperation. I explained what I was doing and why I was doing it. Some of the kids asked if they could help. I not so politely declined their offer and told them that the most helpful thing they could do would be to leave me alone so I could finish before my dad got home.

They shrugged their shoulders, put their hands in their pockets, and shuffled away, glancing back at me with a "Why are you being such a jerk?" look. At that moment I really did not care—I just wanted to get the plants in before Dad arrived.

After over an hour of digging in the hard-packed, heavy clay soil, I had dug all five holes. Each one was eighteen inches deep and three times the width of the roots, so that the holes almost touched one another. I then carefully mixed the dirt, compost, and peat moss in the proper proportions and planted the rosebushes, making sure they were all exactly twenty-four inches from the front walk and exactly twenty-four inches from each other. I remember looking at the roses from every angle and deciding they looked perfectly symmetrical. As I stood there admiring my creation, I heard my dad's car pull up and realized I had not yet put the mulch around the roses. I dropped to my knees and began quickly spreading the mulch so the roses would have that finished look.

As Dad walked up to me, he looked at the roses and then at me and asked, "What in the h--- are you doing?" The tone and intensity of his question shocked me and left me struggling for breath. My response bordered on incoherent as I stammered out something about, "The rut . . . the roses . . . stop the kids from walking here." He stood staring at the roses, silent and frowning. Finally, he said, "They look crooked to me."

As he walked away and into the house, I stayed there on my knees, trying to comprehend what had just happened. *Why do I feel so foolish and weak?* In my passion to do something meaningful for my dad and our home, I had made myself very vulnerable. I was angry at myself for not anticipating his response.

I haphazardly scattered a bit more mulch around the bushes, wanting desperately to still care about the roses, to care about what I was doing. But it was as if my passion to make our home more beautiful had shriveled up in the toxicity of my dad's words. I picked up the leftover packaging and supplies and angrily threw it all in the trash. I never planted another thing in that yard. And my father never said another word about it.

Clearly, my father missed an opportunity to affirm one

of his children. So how significant was that moment? As an adult, I realize my love for growing plants never went away. It connects me somehow to God and the wonder of His creation, and I've always drawn energy from it. I have a deep sense of contentment and peace when I'm surrounded by living, growing things—which is why, when I had an office at Gallup, I filled it with plants and relished the view from my windows, overlooking the Missouri River. I believe that if my father had affirmed and blessed me the day I planted those roses, I most likely would have chosen a career in horticulture.

I do not blame my father for the career path I chose; I am the one who tossed out everything having to do with gardening and landscaping. I understand that my father and I were not at all alike. Our differences seemed to completely confound him and, as a result, to irritate and anger him. Nevertheless, the story of the rosebushes shows just what power a word of blessing—or a lack of one—has in directing and shaping a life.

And what do I mean when I talk about the word *blessing*? For most people, a blessing is something you give before a meal or when someone sneezes. Many people may say things like, "You are such a blessing" or "That was a blessing" when referring to a positive event in their lives. However, such uses don't convey the transforming power inherent in the way I am using the word. When speaking the language of blessing, a person communicates, affirms, and empowers God-given intrinsic attributes—such as personality, gifting, talents, character traits, and intelligences—that he or she sees in another person.

Sadly, I hadn't learned the language of blessing by the time I was a dad myself. I often took on a critical, glass-is-half-empty approach with my own sons. When I asked them to do something in the yard or around the house, I inspected their efforts and pointed out what did not meet my expectations—expectations I now realize I'd either communicated poorly or failed to communicate at all.

*When you speak the language of blessing, you communicate, affirm, and empower God-given intrinsic attributes that you see in another person.*

✦ ✦ ✦

When my wife would overhear me scolding one of the boys, she'd sometimes point out that she had not heard me clearly explain those standards to my sons. I would then say something like, "I should not have to point out that kind of detail. Any fool would know that is the way it needs to be done."

My focus was always on what needed improvement. Like most people, I found it very difficult to give to others what I had not received from my own dad.

It does not have to be like that. In the introduction, I explained how New Life, a ministry in which I helped people through relational challenges, taught me the importance of unconditional love and acceptance. It was also the first time I learned how intrinsically the blessing is tied to whether you and I feel affirmed.

My experiences at New Life also enabled me to see the reality of my life as a child and as a young adult. I had always tried to portray myself as the product of an idealistic,

Midwestern, middle-class experience. The reality was something very different. My father tried to be a good man, but he struggled with alcoholism and inappropriate anger. At times he felt such rage that he became physically abusive and demanded perfection. He also struggled with a bipolar disorder. I have calculated that, by the time I left home at age twenty, I had received over ten thousand statements of criticism from him and not a single word of affirmation. I believe my father had the distorted belief that if you praise a child, he will quit trying to improve. Criticism, not praise, he thought, would make a person stronger.

In his later years, when my dad was suffering from asbestosis, I would sit by his chair or bedside. By this point, I was involved in New Life Ministries and had found that I no longer needed or sought his approval. Dad seemed to realize this, which made it much easier for him to relax around me. In addition to telling him about my work and family, I occasionally shared with him what I was learning through my journey with New Life. I think I was hoping that he might find some comfort in these truths.

Because of his labored breathing, talking had become difficult for him. He would listen silently, his eyes full of deep sadness. When I finished, he would just look up and nod his head, usually saying nothing. I interpreted his silence and the nod as affirmation. One day, he suggested I invite my siblings to participate in New Life. That was the closest he ever came to telling me I had done something worthwhile.

I now know he wanted to affirm the God-given blessing

in me, but he had no experience or language to express it. He had not received such a blessing from his father either. I believe his lifelong inability to affirm his children tormented him until his final moments.

No parent should have to experience what my father went through.

## YOU ARE BLESSED

*Today I have given you the choice between life and death, between blessings and curses. Now I call on heaven and earth to witness the choice you make. Oh, that you would choose life, so that you and your descendants might live!* (Deuteronomy 30:19)

Your words bring forth life or death. That may sound melodramatic or overstated; I assure you it is not. What you say has the power to give life to dreams and callings—or to snuff them out before they have a chance to develop.

As Jesus said, "The thief comes only in order to steal and kill and destroy" (John 10:10, AMP). One of the ways the thief (Satan) steals, kills, and destroys is through deceitful words. No wonder, then, that the tongue has the power of life and death.

*What you say has the power to give life to dreams and callings— or to snuff them out before they have a chance to develop.*

✦ ✦ ✦

Fortunately, God's desire for each one of us is life: "I came that they may have and enjoy life, and have it in

abundance (to the full, till it overflows)" (John 10:10, AMP).
In fact, the Bible has a great deal to say about blessings;
it mentions *blessing* or derivative terms over four hundred
times! There are three Greek words in the New Testament
related directly to the English word *blessing*:

- *Eulogeitos* is an adjective meaning "well spoken of;
  praised."
- *Eulogew* is a verb meaning "to speak well of; to
  praise; to call down God's gracious power."
- *Eulogia* is a noun meaning "praise; fine speaking."

Although these words are Greek, the original language
of the New Testament, the concept of blessing is completely
Hebrew in origin, starting in the first book of the Bible.
In Genesis we read about God blessing Abram (whom He
would soon rename Abraham):

*The LORD had said to Abram, "Go from your country,*
*your people and your father's household to the land I*
*will show you.*

*"I will make you into a great nation,*
    *and I will bless you;*
*I will make your name great,*
    *and you will be a blessing.*
*I will bless those who bless you,*
    *and whoever curses you I will curse;*
*and all peoples on earth*
    *will be blessed through you."*

*So Abram went, as the LORD had told him; and Lot went with him. Abram was seventy-five years old when he set out from Harran. He took his wife Sarai, his nephew Lot, all the possessions they had accumulated and the people they had acquired in Harran, and they set out for the land of Canaan, and they arrived there.* (Genesis 12:1-5, NIV)

I see four key principles about the blessing in this brief passage:

1. All blessings originate from God.
2. We are never too old to receive the blessing.
3. The blessing requires that we take a journey of discovery that will be different from our parents' journeys. We can receive the blessing through our parents, but it will be different from what our parents received.
4. We are blessed so that we can be a blessing to others. Note that God mentions this twice: verse 2 says, "you will be a blessing"; verse 3 goes on to say, "all peoples on earth will be blessed through you." So we see that Abraham would himself be a blessing to others, and through him, the ultimate blessing of Jesus would come to "all peoples on earth."

Every person has already received the blessing from God in the form of his or her unique design, which perfectly corresponds with God's calling for that person's life. Thank goodness this affirmation originates from God, not from our parents!

Yet this gift lies dormant in each of us until it is recognized and affirmed—in other words, until someone speaks the language of blessing into our lives. God's original plan was that His blessing would first be acknowledged by our parents. However, in this fallen world there are no perfectly functional families. If our parents are unable to speak the language of blessing, God does not give up. He finds other people—possibly someone in our extended family, a teacher, a friend, sometimes even a complete stranger—to be a conduit of His blessing to us.

My fifth grade teacher tried to do that for me. She was very tall and thin, her skin so pale it was almost an alabaster white. I suspect she was ill a good part of the time as she walked slowly and labored to breathe, but what I noticed most was her kind expression and gentle smile whenever she looked at me.

One day after class she told me about a writing contest to celebrate Presidents' Day. She encouraged me to enter because she believed I could win. I was incredulous—me, win a writing contest? I didn't think so. Then she asked if I would do it for her. I could not turn her down. I would write the article for her so she would receive recognition as a great teacher.

Imagine my shock when my story won first place. My mom was excited about the award, but neither she nor my father attended the award ceremony. My picture was in the paper, but I did not care. I was sure my win was a fluke. Since it didn't impress my father, it meant nothing to me either. I missed the affirmation God wanted me to have because I was demanding that it come through my father.

By age ten, I had become the primary hindrance to receiving the blessing in my life, which meant I would be unable to pass it on to anyone else. After all, you cannot give to others what you have not received yourself. Only through New Life did I learn that accessing the blessing for myself was not conditional upon receiving my father's approval, which had seemed so impossible to earn.

Not only does God's blessing communicate our purpose, our meaning, and our reason for existence, it influences how we relate to others and how others will relate to us. It is indelibly a part of our very identity and our destiny. It has the authority and power of God to transform our lives. It speaks to each person's true authentic self; it empowers and releases God's unique design, calling, and purpose in our lives.

*You cannot give to others what you have not received yourself.*

Blessings are prophetic in that they communicate the heart, mind, and will of God for an individual. They connect us with our Creator's dream for us. Words of blessing affirm and empower God-given intrinsic attributes, such as personality, gifting, talents, character traits, and intelligences.

When we hear a blessing from God through another person, it resonates deep within our hearts, our innermost beings. We recognize that the words are true and authentic, and they speak the truth about who we were created to be. It touches a deep passion within each of us to make a difference in this world.

*The blessing connects us with our Creator's dream for us.*

✦ ✦ ✦

## THE POWER OF WORDS OF AFFIRMATION

Sociologists report that even the average introverted person, if he or she lives to about eighty years old, will influence over ten thousand people. An insurance company produced a TV commercial that illustrates the power of one act of kindness. The ad shows a person doing something kind while another person observes her. The next scene shows the observer doing a kind deed, which is then observed by someone else, who then does his own act of kindness. You get the gist; it is an illustration of a kind of pay-it-forward concept.

Notice that it wasn't just one person, the observer, who was influenced. The first person's act of kindness acted as a catalyst to all the other people's acts of kindness. In a way, then, that first person was actually "responsible" for the actions that followed. The more I ponder this, the more I conclude that the estimate that even one introvert influences ten thousand people is probably much too conservative.

If you doubt that you and I really have that much influence, consider what happened to me not long ago when I walked into our local gas station to pick up a fountain drink. As I proceeded to the counter, deep in thought about the next chapter of this book, the attendant behind the counter exclaimed, "Ah! What's the matter?"

His pained response shocked me out of my preoccupation. I looked at him and said, "Huh?" He said, "Joe, you always come in here with a smile on your face, and you always greet us. Today you walked in without so much as a 'Hi,' and you looked almost angry."

Now, I was not angry at all; when I am deep in thought, though, I must look angry. What so caught my attention was how strongly the attendant reacted to my not greeting him and smiling as usual. It was another example of how we influence and bless people.

A more poignant example comes from a good friend, whom I'll call Mary. While we discussed how affirming people's gifts and talents is a powerful way to bless one another, she told me how she'd witnessed this for herself.

One day at work, Mary sat down at a lunch table opposite Betty, a coworker whom everyone tried to avoid. Betty always seemed down, and she was cranky and very unpleasant to be around. Mary couldn't help wondering, since everyone has gifts and talents, what Betty's looked like. As Mary thought about it, she recalled many of the skills and talents Betty exhibited in her work, some of which directly benefited Mary.

As she began eating her salad, Mary said, "Betty, I wanted

to tell you how much I appreciate the way you . . ." As Mary proceeded to articulate each of Betty's positive contributions at work, her coworker sat speechless, tears filling her eyes. Finally, she told Mary that it had been a very long time since anyone had said anything kind to her.

Betty began to tell Mary how she had spent all her life caring for others. As a young girl, she cared for her sickly mother. Now she was caring for her husband, who was too ill to work. Betty continually felt overwhelmed and trapped. Though life had not been kind to Betty, when Mary spoke life and blessing to her, it had a profound influence.

One final example of the power we have to bless one another comes from the movie *Hugo*, which I recently enjoyed watching with my family. The story revolves around a young boy named Hugo who loves to fix things—especially clocks.

Hugo's mother has died; his father is a watchmaker who works in a museum fixing complicated devices. Hugo loves spending time with his father learning the trade. At the beginning of the movie, Hugo's father is trying to repair an enormously complicated mechanical boy, an automaton that has been donated to the museum.

Tragically, Hugo's father dies in a fire at the museum. Without any compassion, Hugo's drunken uncle arrives at Hugo's home to tell the boy that his father is dead. He then drags Hugo to the train station, where the uncle lives and works maintaining the clocks. Before leaving his home, the only thing Hugo grabs is the automaton, which he intends to repair someday. Meanwhile, Hugo learns his uncle's trade of keeping the station's clocks running.

Even after his uncle disappears, Hugo continues to live at the station and maintain the clocks. There he befriends a young girl who was adopted by her godparents. Together they try to solve the mystery of the automaton, which Hugo thinks carries a secret message for him from his father. Hugo believes this message will speak to his very purpose in life.

This brings me to what I consider the key point of the movie: a conversation between the two children about their life's purpose. Hugo says, "If you lose your purpose, it's like you're broken." He adds, "I'd imagine the whole world was one big machine. Machines never come with any extra parts, you know. They always come with the exact amount they need. So I figured, if the entire world was one big machine, I couldn't be an extra part. I had to be here for some reason. And that means you have to be here for some reason too."[1]

"If you lose your purpose, it's like you're broken." Wow, what an insight! So many people feel broken because they do not know their true and authentic purpose in life. Film reviewer Drew McWeeny observed about *Hugo*, "Early on, it's obvious that the film is less about the mechanical man and more about the way broken people sometimes need other people to fix them, how we can all play some part in the lives of others, sometimes without meaning to."[2]

*So many people feel broken because they do not know their true and authentic purpose in life.*

✦ ✦ ✦

I am quite passionate about several concepts underscored by this movie:

1. We are created with purpose.
2. When we have lost our purpose, it is as if we are broken, and we do not function the way our Creator designed us to function.
3. Sometimes we need other people to help fix us— to help us find our true purpose—an illustration of our interdependency.
4. We often play a part in the lives of others, sometimes without even being aware of it. The more we can live with a clear sense of purpose, the more impact and influence we will have on others.

You are not an accident. Before He even created the world, God began to dream of you. The apostle Paul writes, "Even before he made the world, God loved us and chose us in Christ to be holy and without fault in his eyes. God decided in advance to adopt us into his own family by bringing us to himself through Jesus Christ" (Ephesians 1:4-5).

He envisioned a unique design for you and decided to invite you and your purpose into His eternal purposes. That purpose will not end with your physical death. After you've finished your life on planet Earth, you will stand before our Lord and Maker. If you've lived out your purpose, you can expect to hear these words: "Well done, my good and faithful servant" (Matthew 25:21).

**APPLICATION ACTIVITY**

I serve as a life coach to a number of individuals and couples. Life coaching is very different from sports coaching, voice coaching, and even executive or business coaching. In those areas, coaches are viewed as the experts in their fields and tell others what they are to do. In life coaching, I do little instructing; instead, I ask lots of questions. That's because I understand that each individual I coach is the world's leading "expert" on his or her unique design and calling. Through the right questions, I help draw out what is deep within each person into his or her conscious awareness. I then affirm and celebrate each person's unique design.

I have coached over one thousand highly gifted and talented individuals, and I have noticed that when we start working together, the vast majority have little or no sense of their life's mission. When I ask them about their "unique" purpose, many roll their eyes and ask, "Really, a unique purpose? You're serious? I'm supposed to have one?" You may feel the same way at this point. I understand. Many people find it extremely difficult to discover their distinctive purpose on their own. As you will learn in part 2, this can be challenging for many reasons. The good news, explained in part 3, is that there are many tools to help you discover it.

As you begin this book, let me assure you that the benefits

of knowing your unique design and purpose are numerous. If the idea of finding your life purpose seems out of reach right now, I encourage you to work through the Application Activities at the end of each chapter. Writing down or discussing your answers to the questions will put you on the path to discovering the gifts and purpose God has placed within you. Knowing what you were put on earth to do will then positively affect your relationships, your work, your spirituality, your health, and every other area of your life.

1.  Do you have a sense of your unique purpose—what you were born to do?

2.  If you do have a sense of your distinctive purpose, how would you describe it? If you don't, what is your response to the assertion that you, like every other person, were designed with a God-given purpose in mind?

*Chapter 2*

# WE ARE HIS WORKMANSHIP

A great artist once contributed one of his masterpieces to a small community. This piece was unique and showed great complexity and sophistication. It was also a perfect representation of the passion and profound love the master brought to each of his works.

The townspeople reacted with great excitement as they anticipated getting their first glimpse of this masterpiece, and almost everyone came to the unveiling. When it was finally uncovered, the room was filled with oohs and aahs. The people marveled at what they agreed had to be one of the master's most beautiful creations, and laughter and tears of wonder conveyed their deep joy. They were so proud that this work of art had been given to their community.

After a while, though, something very strange began

to happen. One of the townspeople decided he could improve the masterpiece just by adding a tiny dab of yellow here and there. When people noticed what he'd done, they, too, began to make very small additions. At first, they were hardly noticeable, but as more and more people began to make these small, seemingly insignificant additions, the painting's appearance began to change. Some people did not like what others had done and decided they could correct it by adding their own strokes.

People no longer oohed and aahed when they saw this masterpiece. They would cock their heads slightly, perplexed as they pondered this work and observed that something just wasn't quite right. Some even questioned how the master could call this one of his great creations. By now, the master's original work had become completely obscured by all the "tiny" dabs the community people had added. An authentic masterpiece had been covered up by inauthentic additions. What a tragic loss!

It's unthinkable that any museum would allow such vandalizing of a work of art. None of us would condone such outrageous behavior. But this story is an allegory of what we do to one another every day, even to our own loved ones. Without understanding that each person has been created with the Master's specific plan, often parents, teachers, coworkers, and other people decide to add a dab here and a dab there. The uniqueness of many human masterpieces is almost completely obscured by the time many young people reach their early twenties.

With the best of intentions, we often try to get people to conform to the standards we think best, rather than affirming the unique ways in which God has shaped them. Yet it's impossible to speak the language of blessing—to affirm and empower people's intrinsic attributes—while we're trying to make them over.

I once coached a youth pastor who had always felt called to ministry. As a young boy, he sensed God's presence almost everywhere he looked—in a beautiful sky, in a forest, in a young family in the park. Because he felt God's presence so often, prayer with God came naturally. As a new youth pastor, each time he would see or even think of a particular child, he would lift that young person up in prayer. This brought him great joy, and he felt very close to each of the children he served and even closer to God.

*With the best of intentions, we often try to get people to conform to the standards we think best, rather than affirming the unique ways in which God has shaped them.*

✦ ✦ ✦

Then at a staff meeting one morning, the senior pastor gave a brief talk on the importance of all the pastors praying for those in their area of ministry. The senior pastor told them how, early every morning, he would pray for their church, for each of the staff, and for the congregation. Everyone understood the goodness of the pastor's actions, and they all nodded in affirmation. Then, without warning, the senior pastor turned to the youth pastor and said, in a very pointed, almost angry tone, "And if I ever find out that you are not spending one to two hours every morning in prayer for our kids, I will fire you on the spot!" Then the senior pastor gave a little laugh and smiled at the rest of the staff. As he went on to conduct the meeting as if nothing had happened, the youth pastor was left to wonder if the pastor had made the comment in jest. Or did the pastor really believe he didn't pray for the church's youth?

Everyone on staff knew that the senior pastor was an early riser with a very structured routine. A regular early-morning prayer time fit him perfectly. The youth pastor, however, had never been a morning person, yet he offered heartfelt prayers for the youth intermittently all day long. Now he felt expected to wake early for a more structured time of prayer. What had been so effortless, so natural for him now felt . . . lifeless, as if God were no longer listening. As time passed, it also became more difficult for him to pray spontaneously. Then the youth pastor began to question whether he was called to ministry after all. Eventually he resigned his position.

Months later he had a brief meeting with the senior pastor, where he tried to explain how the older man's comments had affected him. The pastor dismissed it by saying, "You just don't understand how I show people I care about them." Sadly, this leader did not realize that admonishing his staff to be more like him was not caring for them.

How often has something similar been done to you? How many people have tried to change you without first getting to know and appreciate who you truly are? How many people just assume they know what is best for you?

When I speak on this concept, the question I hear most

often is, "How in the world can I actually know God's plan for myself, let alone for other people?" My response is that it is a process and a journey. I believe we have always carried our calling in our hearts, but we each need other people to help draw out and affirm God's special purpose for us. As our understanding of our own unique design and purpose grows stronger and clearer, we will begin helping others discover their own callings. As we mature, we naturally "give preference to one another" (Romans 12:10, NASB).

Preferring one another requires what family therapist Edwin Friedman called a nonanxious presence. In his classic book on family systems, *Generation to Generation*, Friedman explains that people with a nonanxious presence are calm, nonjudgmental, lighthearted, and at peace in their own skins with no personal agendas. They have a sense of meaning and purpose, and a deep gratitude for who God has uniquely created them to be. As a result, they are free to give their attention completely to another, to see and appreciate the uniqueness in that other person.[1]

A touching scene from the movie *The Help* illustrates this principle so well. After little Mae Mobley Leefolt's mother has been unfairly critical of her young toddler, the Leefolts' maid, Aibileen, holds Mae Mobley gently on her lap. Aibileen then looks directly into the little girl's eyes and says, "You is kind. You is smart. You is important." Later on, after Mae Mobley's mother fires Aibileen, we hear the little girl softly tell herself, "You is kind. You is smart. You is important."[2] She has received the blessing from Aibileen.

Until someone speaks blessing, affirmation, and encouragement, acknowledging your gifts and uniqueness, these things just do not become "real" to you. With one another's help, we discover our gifts and our God-given design, and we are pointed in the direction of God's purpose and calling in our lives.

## YOU ARE GIFTED—AND SO ARE YOUR LOVED ONES

God created you from a palette of endless possibilities. To consider just how rich this variety is, let's focus exclusively on spiritual gifts for a moment. In several of their New Testament letters, the apostles Peter and Paul list some of the spiritual gifts we can receive from the Holy Spirit. (See Romans 12, 1 Corinthians 12, Ephesians 4, and 1 Peter 4.) They never, however, provide an exhaustive or comprehensive list. I believe that was intentional. They understood the incredible diversity of those who make up the community of the faithful.

*Until someone acknowledges your gifts and uniqueness, they just do not become "real" to you.*

✦ ✦ ✦

In this book, we'll consider four other areas that contribute to each person's genius:

- personality
- talents

- intelligence
- character and virtues

These characteristics, combined with your life circumstances, make you different from everyone else who has ever walked the earth. As Dr. Caroline Leaf, a neuroplasticity scientist and author, says, "Your gift is the missing piece. It's always an answer and never a problem. It is unique, intentional, having a purpose, design and measurable structure."[3]

Later on, I'll introduce you to proven assessments you can use to discover your strengths in your personality, talents, intelligence, and character. As with spiritual gifts, there is incredible diversity within these four categories.

## ONE OF A KIND

Add experiences, education, and other differences to the four categories above, and you'll see why I say you are unique. No one exactly like you has ever existed or will ever exist again. You have a one-of-a-kind gift to offer to the world. If you do not identify, develop, and contribute these strengths, the world will be weaker because it will miss out on your gift. The same is true for each of your loved ones.

Let's think back to three-year-old Mae Mobley from the movie *The Help*. The little girl desperately needs encouragement, something her mother seems unable to give her. Aibileen combines her gift of encouragement with an ability to articulate words of strength and confidence: "You is kind. You is smart. You is important." In this way, she speaks words of blessing on Mae Mobley. Yet another natural encourager might be an empathetic listener who could bless Mae Mobley by validating her hurt and promising to be there to listen whenever Mae Mobley needs her. This is an example of how the gift of encouragement may be expressed very differently by two unique people.

*If you do not identify and develop your strengths, the world will be weaker because it will miss out on your gift.*

✦ ✦ ✦

When seeking biblical counsel on parenting, we often turn to Proverbs 22:6: "Train up a child in the way he should go, even when he is old he will not depart from it" (NASB). Unfortunately, reading it this way means we lose much of its significance and misunderstand God's intentions about how we are to respond to one another.

In our culture, parents often see their children as blank slates. Or they see them as similar to lumps of formless clay just waiting for enlightened hands to mold them into what they should become. This approach to parenting is called Western determinism and places a heavy emphasis on nurture. As you can tell, it pays little attention to—or even downplays altogether—each child's nature, or innate uniqueness.

Let's examine another translation of Proverbs 22:6: "Train up a child in the way he should go [and in keeping with his individual gift or bent], and when he is old he will not depart from it" (AMP).

That little addition—"in keeping with his individual gift or bent"—makes a big difference, doesn't it? Apparently God is intentional in the way He forms each child and how that child is designed to function. Science confirms this. Each child is born with a unique neural map, with predispositions for gifts and talents, an innate genius just waiting to be developed.

The point here is that we must discover and draw out what God has already placed within each child and each person. That's why, as Dr. Caroline Leaf says, "Let's just begin to realize at this point that genius is in all of us when we use our gifts."[4]

Don't get me wrong: I am not suggesting that parents should be permissive with their children when it comes to teaching values, good manners, and social skills; however, we do need to discover and honor the masterpieces God created. We must remember that even our kids' values, manners, and social skills will be dramatically impacted by their unique design. My five sons exhibit a broad spectrum of human personality, talents, and gifts, ranging from gregarious and very social to introverted and quiet, from avant-garde to straight arrow, from Regents Scholar to special needs. In short, they are dramatically different from each other. Yet each one exhibits good manners and is courteous, respectful, kind, and generous. Their mother actually deserves most of the credit for that.

The sad reality today is that the vast majority of people are unaware of the gifts they have received from their Creator—or even that they were uniquely created by God.

In fact, Gallup research shows that we generally focus more on "correcting" the weaknesses in ourselves and others—what we are not—than on developing our strengths—who we are: unique masterpieces with God as the artist.[5] In *StrengthsFinder 2.0*, Tom Rath laments the way our "fixation on deficits affects young people in the home and classroom. In every culture we have studied, the overwhelming majority of parents (77% in the United States) think that a student's *lowest* grades deserve the *most* time and attention. Parents and teachers reward excellence with apathy instead of investing more time in the areas where a child has the most potential for greatness."[6]

Consider the child who brings home her report card from school. She has three As, a B+, and a D. How will her parents react? Most likely, they will virtually ignore the four subjects in which she is clearly talented. Even loving parents are likely to say something like, "Honey, it's great that you got three As, but what is going on with this D? We are going to have to really focus on getting that up to at least a B! Do you understand me?"

Clearly, that statement is not spoken in the language of blessing. What the child quickly realizes is that her focus should not be on what she loves to do, what she excels in, and what she truly enjoys; instead, she should pour her energies into what she is not, what she struggles with.

As a result, the child will most likely have to put far more energy into bringing that D up to a B than she had to expend to get the three As.

That's largely because, in our culture, we emphasize the importance of being well rounded; it is more important to try to be above average in all subjects than to excel in some. However, we were not created to be jacks-of-all-trades and masters of none; we were created to excel differently and discriminately. Each child has a unique set of gifts and talents. You may be thinking, *Now, wait a minute. It is not okay for my child to bring home a D; at a minimum, the child needs to be competent in that subject.* You are probably right. But what if the conversation went something like this: "You got three As and a B+! I am so proud of you. Tell me, what do you enjoy about each of these subjects?" As the child articulates what she loves about each of them, the parents can begin to remember times they noticed their child's enjoyment of similar activities and subjects. The more they can affirm the child by recalling specific times she exhibited these talents and intelligences, the better.

After affirming the child in this way, they could then say, "Tell me about the D." And then, "How can I help you with this subject?" The B+ subject is a kind of low-hanging fruit for the child and probably would require only a little bit of extra effort to get an A. The parents might even follow their discussion on the D by saying something like, "You are clearly very good in this B+ subject; what might you need to do to get an A? I think with that little extra effort you could have four As. What do you think?"

## A BETTER WAY

Jesus said that He came in order to give us "a rich and satisfying life" (John 10:10). Or as the King James Version puts it, "I am come that they might have life, and that they might have it more abundantly." As Christians, we should embrace this abundance mentality. We are to focus on what God has given to us out of His lavish abundance. Our gifts and talents were freely given to us, primarily as a means to benefit others. In fact, a growing body of research shows that humans experience our greatest joy when we meaningfully contribute something of significant value to others out of our unique gifts and talents.

*You and I experience our greatest joy when we meaningfully contribute to others out of our unique gifts and talents.*

Too often, though, we behave like the townspeople observing the artist's masterpiece who decide they can improve on the great artist's work. But interfering with God's plan for others, particularly young people, to shine in the sphere of their giftedness is damaging. When we continually focus on what our children are not, they are likely to become fear-based adults, trying to hold on to what "little" they have, while always looking to get more. They develop a scarcity mentality.

Instead, as adults, we are to recognize and then try to draw out the innate genius of each child. Admittedly that is a very time-consuming process that often feels inefficient for the adults in the child's life. It requires great patience.

Pastor and leadership blogger Dan Rockwell reminds us to be patient when encouraging others to grow and develop:

1. Patience is trusting—believing in—the potential of others.
2. Patience is humbly holding back *your* knowing in order to facilitate the knowing of others and then celebrating *their* growth. It never says, "I knew that."
3. Patience confidently says, "You have more in you."[7]

Patience, in other words, is looking at the masterpiece that is our child, our coworker, or our spouse and, rather than trying to improve on the master's work, admiring—perhaps even oohing and aahing over—that person's unique design.

APPLICATION ACTIVITY

The allegory of the masterpiece at the beginning of this chapter resonates with many of the people I coach.

1. Can you recall a time when someone of influence in your life tried to add a "dab of paint" on you? He or she was likely trying to get you to embrace something that you knew was not an authentic part of who you are. It may

have been expressed in sentences like those below. You fill in the blanks:

"You need to be more _____."

"You should always _____!"

"Why don't you _____ more than you do?"

2. What did it feel like to hear such comments? How did you respond?

3. How might those words be affecting you today?

# Chapter 8

# GOD SPEAKS THE LANGUAGE OF BLESSING

To look for and then point out the glimpses of masterpiece you see in your child, your coworker, or even a stranger is to speak God's language. Few people truly grasp how much God knows them, unconditionally accepts them, loves them, and has so abundantly blessed them.

While I was meeting with a new group of New Life participants years ago, I met a woman who did not grasp God's love for her. I can still remember the first time I met Susan, a petite, almost frail woman with long, brown hair. She was very quiet and stared at the floor during most of our meeting.

When it came time to share her story, she said, "I have

ruined my life and my family's lives. I drove away my husband, and now my children won't even talk to me. As far as God is concerned, I know He is angry with me and doesn't like me—He might even hate me. And who could blame Him? I have destroyed my life, and I am hopeless."

As I listened to Susan, I could not imagine what this dear, gentle woman could have done that led her to believe that even God hated her. As I got to know her better, I discovered the only thing she was guilty of was denying her family her true self. Her husband was a highly self-confident man who had strong expectations of who his wife needed to be. As you might guess, his expectations had virtually nothing in common with who she truly was. The more she tried to be the person he demanded her to be, the worse he treated her and the less he respected her. She so wanted to please her children that she tried as hard as she could to make them happy, to the point of near physical exhaustion. But they began to show the same disdain and disrespect her husband so often showed her. The more she tried to make them happy, the weaker her family thought she was. She had completely lost herself in an avalanche of unfounded expectations. She was clearly in a state of clinical depression.

Like other twelve-step programs, New Life encouraged participants to be honest and vulnerable and, in turn, provided a nonjudgmental environment in which participants could express themselves authentically. As Susan began to open up, she revealed parts of who she really was. Unlike her family, who made her feel condemned for not living up to their unfounded expectations, her small group affirmed her, telling her, "We really like the way you show compassion to other people." In this nurturing environment, her small group witnessed a startling transformation. No longer was she a dowdy-looking, dull-eyed woman; instead, she exuded a calm, yet strong presence.

Fast-forward two years from my first meeting with Susan. This lovely woman was now almost radiant in her enthusiasm and energy, completely at peace with herself and with God. As she told me where God was leading her, I was astonished. She was going to take over a small orphanage in a third-world country, inspired by another petite woman, a nun from Albania, who had also been greatly underestimated. I asked her if she had ever lived in a foreign country, though I already knew the answer. She told me no, other than the two weeks she had spent visiting this orphanage. Yet once she realized how poorly the kids in this orphanage were being treated, her compassion ignited a righteous anger and determination to provide a loving and safe environment for these oppressed children.

Now, many years later, I can report that this woman served in that orphanage for nearly two decades. During that time, she reconciled with her children, who were amazed by the incredible faith and strength she possessed. Rather than desperately trying to meet everyone else's expectations, she offered her unique gifts and the blessing of her peaceful presence.

Susan is also now able to rest in the certainty that God

loves and delights in her, just as He loves every child she works with. In this way, she is much like King David, known as "a man after God's own heart," who also understood the innate worth in every person. Though, like all of us, he was a man of many frailties and weaknesses, David passionately loved God and knew he was loved by God. Perhaps this is nowhere better expressed than in Psalm 139. Notice how David's gratitude for God's love permeates every verse.

> *You have searched me, LORD,*
>     *and you know me.*
> *You know when I sit and when I rise;*
>     *you perceive my thoughts from afar.*
> *You discern my going out and my lying down;*
>     *you are familiar with all my ways.*
> *Before a word is on my tongue*
>     *you, LORD, know it completely.* (Psalm 139:1-4, NIV)

"You . . . know everything about me" (Psalm 139:1, NLT). David knew such intimacy with God. He was aware that God knew him and perceived his every thought, word, and action. There is no sense of arrogance in David's words, but rather childlike wonder that he is so known, accepted, and loved by God.

When I was growing up, my grandparents were my favorite people. Now that I am a grandparent myself, I realize that the way we unconditionally accept and celebrate every achievement of our grandchildren reflects the way

God wants to celebrate our lives. When I am watching my grandson play baseball, his stats become meaningless. We will find something to celebrate, no matter what the score. And when he hears my wife and me celebrate him in that way, his eyes fill with delight. He knows that he is known, accepted, loved, and yes, even celebrated.

In Psalm 139:13-16 (NIV) David attributes the beauty of each person not to the individual but to the Creator.

> *For you created my inmost being;*
> > *you knit me together in my mother's womb.*
> *I praise you because I am fearfully and wonderfully made;*
> > *your works are wonderful,*
> > *I know that full well.*

Out of his deep and profound sense of gratitude, David says, "I am fearfully and wonderfully made." What a great expression of healthy self-esteem!

> *My frame was not hidden from you*
> > *when I was made in the secret place,*
> > *when I was woven together in the depths of the earth.*
> *Your eyes saw my unformed body;*
> > *all the days ordained for me were written in your book*
> > *before one of them came to be.*

David knew that God had ordained a plan for his life and that He was intimately involved in all the details. Can there be the slightest doubt that David knew God created him as an individual with a unique calling and purpose? That God had abundantly blessed him? You and I speak the language of blessing not by downplaying God's good gifts to us but by looking for and then acknowledging the ways others are fearfully and wonderfully made.

*We speak the language of blessing when we look for and then acknowledge the ways others are fearfully and wonderfully made.*

✦ ✦ ✦

In the New Testament Jesus gets at the truth of God's intimate awareness of each person in another way. While telling His followers not to fear those who oppose them, He says, "Are not two sparrows sold for a penny? Yet not one of them will fall to the ground outside your Father's care. And even the very hairs of your head are all numbered" (Matthew 10:29-30, NIV). God so loves you, He knows the very number of the hairs on your head! Unimaginable but true. Oh, how He knows you and loves you!

God's love for each person is also expressed through Jesus' parable of the Good Shepherd, who left the ninety-nine sheep of his flock to find and save the one lost lamb. (See Matthew 18:10-14.) What is Jesus' message in this parable? Is it not that God so values each of us that He would leave those who are safe to save the one who is lost?

God's heart is as much on the individual as it is on the collective body. Consider the apostle Paul's understanding of God's heart toward each person on earth, even those who are far from Him. Paul addresses idol-worshiping Greeks in Athens, telling them that God is not far from each of them:

*From one man he made every nation of men, that they should inhabit the whole earth; and he determined the times set for them and the exact places where they should live. God did this so that men would seek him and perhaps reach out for him and find him, though he is not far from each one of us.* (Acts 17:26-27, NIV 1984)

Notice in the last line of the passage above the word *each*, indicating that God is aware of the unique makeup and situation of every individual.

God not only knows and loves each and every person— He knows every person's individual gifts and makeup. Clearly, they were not distributed at random. In the parable of the talents, Jesus tells of a landowner who entrusted each of his servants with a different amount of his riches to invest while he was away: "To one he gave five talents of money, to another two talents, and to another one talent, each according to his ability" (Matthew 25:15, NIV 1984). A talent was a denomination of currency worth the lifetime wages of a laborer, so even the individual who got "only" one talent received the monetary value of a lifetime of work. And he buried it out of fear! What a tragedy.

Each was given neither more nor less than he had the ability to manage. Each would have to give an account of what he did with what the landowner gave him.

Like the three servants, you and I have been given unique gifts from God: "Grace (God's unmerited favor) was given to each of us individually [not indiscriminately, but in different ways] in proportion to the measure of Christ's [rich and bounteous] gift" (Ephesians 4:7, AMP). When we deny God's unmerited favor and the special and unique gifts in ourselves or others, we are essentially burying what God gave us to invest. Whether out of fear or a false sense of pride (masquerading as humility), it's a tragic loss. And I believe that Jesus' parable tells us there are consequences to such behavior.

*When we deny God's unmerited favor and the unique gifts He has given us, we are essentially burying what God gave us to invest.*

✦ ✦ ✦

This unique gift, this blessing of grace, which Jesus has chosen individually for each of us, may be manifested in countless ways in our lives. As we acknowledge the good gifts God has given us, we need to understand two things: First, our gift perfectly aligns with God's dream for us. Second, God's dream for our lives is intended to benefit others. We've each been given a great privilege—a unique calling from our heavenly Father.

Consider Jesus' words as He discusses how individual our reward or lack of reward will be: "The Son of Man is going to come in his Father's glory with his angels, and then he will reward *each person* according to what he has done" (Matthew 16:27, NIV 1984, emphasis mine).

If God will reward each of us based individually and

exclusively on the exercise of our free will, then each of us must possess the freedom and responsibility to make moral decisions as to how we live and how we use the gifts God has given us.

It will not matter who our parents were, nor will it matter who our friends were, what our job was, or what our other circumstances in life were. It will all come down to the fact that each of us had the gift of free will, each of us had access to abundant grace, each of us was gifted and talented, each of us was created with purpose and meaning, and each of us had a calling upon our lives. Each of us was created for a special purpose and designed to hear, "Well done, my good and faithful servant." That is our ultimate destiny.

**APPLICATION ACTIVITY**

"You . . . know everything about me" (Psalm 139:1). The psalmist David's words might be frightening if he were describing anyone other than our loving heavenly Father, who has created each of us with a unique purpose in mind. Unfortunately, most people don't take the time to carefully study and consider the way God has gifted them; as a result, they spend much of their lives futilely trying to meet the expectations of other people.

1. What percentage of the life you are living is your authentic life, the life you were created and called to live? Please do not get hung up on trying to be overly precise here. Just go with your "gut" sense. Some people will respond by saying, "Hardly any." Some will respond with a number like 20 percent or 50 percent. The key here is to determine your perception of how frequently you live out of your authentic self. That's the first step on your journey to a more meaningful and vibrant life.

2. Which of the following best describes how intentional you are in developing your gifts and talents?
   - ☐ I do not even know what my gifts and talents are.
   - ☐ I have taken some assessments (e.g., Myers-Briggs, StrengthsFinder, the VIA) to discover my gifts and talents, but I have no plan in place to develop them.
   - ☐ I have taken some assessments to discover my gifts and talents, and I am working through a plan to develop them.
   - ☐ I have taken some assessments to discover my gifts and strengths, and I am working with a life coach.
   - ☐ I have taken some assessments and have been developing my gifts and talents for years.

Wherever you are on your journey, you'll find ideas on how to discover and develop your gifts in the coming chapters.

*Part 2*

# THE BARRIERS
# TO BLESSING

# Chapter 4

# THE HIGH COST
# OF SEEING YOURSELF
# AS AVERAGE

Nathan Zuckerman, the narrator of the novel *American Pastoral*, is nearly as starstruck at the sight of Swede Levov as he was fifty years before when he was just a kid. Back then, Swede was the standout high school athlete in their community. Swede's younger brother, Jerry, had been a friend of Nathan's, which pulled him into the hometown hero's orbit.

Swede has written Nathan a letter, asking if he'd be willing to meet for lunch to discuss a tribute that Swede wants to write to his father. Nathan, who has become a famous author, agrees. He is intrigued at the chance to find out if there is more to his boyhood idol, now a successful businessman, than the pleasant front he puts forward.

The two men meet at Vincent's, a downtown restaurant where Swede seems as adored by the waitstaff as he was by the residents of the close-knit community in which they grew up. Still, Nathan gets impatient and annoyed as they spend their lunch talking only about Swede's business adventures and beautiful family. Is Swede's life as perfect as it appears? And why did he ask Nathan to meet with him to get professional advice on a writing project that he doesn't even mention over their meal?

Nathan seems to sense that he is missing something, that Swede is not letting him in on the whole story of his life. As he reflects on their meeting, Nathan comments, "The fact remains that getting people right is not what living is all about anyway. It's getting them wrong that is living, getting them wrong and wrong and wrong and then, on careful reconsideration, getting them wrong again. That's how we know we're alive: we're wrong."[1]

Is Nathan right? Will we always get other people "wrong"? After all, later in the novel Nathan finally does uncover the family secrets that Swede tried to keep buried during the last few decades of his life. By that point, however, Swede has died. Should we, like Nathan, accept the impossibility of really knowing someone else?

I don't think so. God clearly intends for every one of us to discover our own gifts and then seek out the distinct gifts in others. For that reason, I don't think it's inevitable that we'll get people wrong all the time. In fact, God gives believers the privilege of speaking life into other people by acknowledging and affirming aspects of their authentic, God-created selves.

At the same time, I think Nathan has a point: most people do not really understand their own identity or that of others. "Ninety per cent of the world's woe," writes journalist Sydney J. Harris, "comes from people not knowing themselves, their abilities, their frailties, and even their real virtues. Most of us go almost all the way through life as complete strangers to ourselves—so how can we know anyone else?"[2]

Harris gets at the root of the problem: if we do not know ourselves, we will never be able to truly know others. A growing body of research identifies self-awareness as one of the foundational attributes to success in one's chosen endeavor in life, especially in leadership roles. "Leaders who do not succeed tend to be people who lack self-awareness. . . . High-performing leaders, however, are aware of their strengths and understand their weaknesses, and see themselves as continuously learning, adapting and responding to both positive and negative circumstances."[3]

> "Most of us go almost all the way through life as complete strangers to ourselves—so how can we know anyone else?"
> SYDNEY J. HARRIS
> ✦ ✦ ✦

In their book *Strengths-Based Leadership*, authors Tom Rath and Barry Conchie recall the importance with which Dr. Don O. Clifton, the father of the Strengths Movement, viewed self-awareness after he had spent years studying leadership:

When Clifton was asked, just a few months before his death in 2003, what his greatest discovery was from three decades of leadership research, this was his response:

A leader needs to know his strengths as a carpenter knows his tools, or as a physician knows the instruments at her disposal. What great leaders have in common is that each truly knows his or her strengths—and can call on the right strength at the right time. This explains why there is no definitive list of characteristics that describes all leaders.[4]

It's not just leaders who don't know themselves very well. The world seems to discourage self-awareness, which comes through discovering our giftedness—our personality, talents, intelligences, character, and calling—and then developing it. Too many people do not know why they do what they do; they just . . . do it.

During the time my five sons were teenagers, I was frequently stunned to hear about some of the destructive behavior of young people in our community. If the bad behavior was done by students whom one of my sons knew from school, I would ask, "What would possess them to do something like that? What were they thinking?"

Each of my sons generally responded in the same way: "They weren't thinking, Dad. They just felt like doing it." Sure, as teenagers mature and grow into young adulthood, they generally exhibit more positive and socially accepted behaviors. However, this maturity is often driven by a desire to avoid negative consequences rather than by growing self-awareness.

How can that be, especially in the Western culture with its emphasis on individualism? We seem to idolize all the individualistic freedoms and rights associated with this philosophy. Yet, in general, our culture encourages us to suppress self-awareness and overemphasize self-freedom. So we see individuals who demand the freedom to do whatever they want to do whenever they want to do it, without the awareness of why they want to do it—they just want to. That is not a good combination.

*Our culture encourages us to suppress self-awareness and overemphasize self-freedom.*

✦ ✦ ✦

So while society gives us free rein to express ourselves, it sometimes appears that there is a great conspiracy to stop us from discovering who we are and what our true purpose and calling are. I believe this process begins in earnest the moment children step into a classroom for the first time.

## *THE ANIMAL SCHOOL*: A FABLE

In the 1940s, a school administrator named George Reavis wrote a call to action on behalf of students everywhere. Surprisingly, he didn't write a report, a newspaper column, or a brochure. Instead he wrote a fable—a simple story about some forest animals who started a school to teach all the animals how to run, swim, fly, and climb. The rabbit was at the top of his class in running but just couldn't master swimming. The eagle excelled at flying and was first to the top of the tree in climbing class but constantly had to be disciplined because he used his own methods to get to the top. The duck was an excellent swimmer and average flyer. Yet he was forced to drop swimming to spend more time in climbing class, which he had flunked. That bothered him but not his teachers because "average was acceptable in school, so nobody worried about that except the duck."[5]

Reavis's story, *The Animal School*, is humorous, but the situation he describes so well is not. When I first heard this tale, it brought back memories of a winter's day when I was in first grade. I vividly remember a discussion my first-grade teacher had with us as she was demonstrating how to make paper snowflakes. She showed us how to fold the paper over several times and then cut various geometric shapes out of the paper. Then, as she unfolded the paper, a beautiful snowflake emerged. As you would guess, each snowflake was somewhat different from all the other paper snowflakes.

Our teacher went on to explain that, just as no two snowflakes are alike, each of us was unique, like the snowflakes we held in our hands. My first thought was *Cool. I like being unique.*

Then, as I started working on my own snowflake, I began to wonder if what she'd said was true. Though I might not have been able to express the source of my uneasiness, I think I already recognized that the teacher treated all of us pretty much the same. She had the same general expectations of us as well.

As I continued in my education, it became increasingly clear that to excel in school we had to comply and conform to the expectations of those in charge. When we did, we were rewarded with gold stars, good grades, smiles of approval from our teachers, and maybe even our classmates' admiration. Failure to comply with the expectations equaled no gold stars, low grades, frowns of disapproval, derision from our classmates, and most likely a serving of corporal punishment at home.

My problem wasn't with my first-grade teacher—or any other teacher, for that matter. I believe the vast majority of teachers pursue education degrees so they can make positive contributions to the lives of children. For many, teaching is not just a job; it is a felt calling.

The current educational system, however, makes it challenging for teachers to affirm students' strengths. Many schools seem, instead, to promote the development of high self-esteem by giving everyone a gold star. Children may feel good initially, but what have they learned about themselves if that affirmation is identical for every student? The rewards, or extrinsic motivators, are expected to affect each student in the same way. No attention is given to our unique intrinsic motivations.

Dr. Leaf makes this observation about what so many have experienced in school:

Unfortunately, one of the most concerning aspects in traditional schooling systems is that some educators are blissfully unaware of the existence of multiple intelligences in their learners. They teach as if all their students' brains process information in exactly the same way.

Students are made to focus on their weaknesses and not given the freedom to focus on their strengths, because educators and parents, most likely through no fault of their own, have no idea what their students' strengths are. In many cases, they may not even acknowledge that some of their students have any strengths at all, especially if they happen not to be strong in Logical/Mathematical and Linguistic domains—the so-called "school intelligences."[6]

The corporate world is not much different from the educational world. Unless employees are superstars in their field of expertise, little recognition is given to their unique characteristics or contributions to the company. The major focus is on their weaknesses, or "opportunities for growth." What most people experience is strong pressure to conform and comply.

*Most people experience strong pressure to conform and comply.*

✦ ✦ ✦

One would hope that home life would be different, and for a lucky few, it is. Some parents do become students of their children and continually celebrate and encourage each child's uniqueness. While they have healthy expectations for their children—that they will respect others, work hard, be kind—these parents do not hold unfounded expectations.

Unfortunately, that is not the norm. Many parents unconsciously pass on to their children the same set of expectations that they were given. They may be well meaning and may themselves spend much of their lives trying to comply with the expectations of others. Now they simply expect the same from their children. After all, they think that is what responsible people do—they try not to disappoint others.

Not only did most of us grow up in homes and schools that expected us to meet certain standards, we have internal voices in our heads that push us to meet a seemingly endless set of expectations. No matter how much or how well we do, it is never quite good enough. Meanwhile, our lives become consumed by busyness even as we become less self-aware, less of who God created us to be.

That is how Swede appears to Nathan in *American Pastoral*. While sitting across from Swede in Vincent's, Nathan silently concludes, "What he has instead of a being . . . is blandness—the guy's radiant with it. He has devised for himself an incognito, and the incognito has become him. . . . Something [has] turned him into a human platitude."[7]

In the next chapter, we'll look at the generational cycle that can be triggered by parents like Swede who have limited self-awareness. Fortunately, we don't need to end up like him. As human beings, we may never be completely self-aware or always loving. Yet as we discover God's unconditional love for us and His gifts and calling in our lives, we can gain a joy beyond human understanding that enables us to live life abundantly, to the full.

APPLICATION ACTIVITY

I was recently coaching a very talented woman who leads teams in various ministry outreaches all over the world. People on her teams frequently say that working with her is a life-changing experience and that she is a great leader. But when I asked her to rate herself as a leader on a scale of 1 to 10, she rated herself a 5!

Then I asked her to describe to me what makes someone a great leader. All her answers were dead-on. And she consistently models these same characteristics and attributes when she leads; however, she struggled to make the connection in her own view of herself. Certainly this woman is humble, but it would not make her less humble to understand that she is gifted and talented. In the end, it is grace—unearned and yet freely and abundantly given—that accounts for her gifts.

The danger in underestimating and undervaluing our true attributes is that it may lead us to disregard or turn down opportunities that beautifully align with our purpose and calling in life. The loss of our unique contributions, the benefits that others miss, and the great joy we forgo are tragic. As long as we know where our gifts came from and we are grateful for them, we can remain humble even as we use them to their fullest.

1. Currently, when it comes to your unique gifts and design, how would you rate your self-awareness?
   ☐ Very self-aware
   ☐ Somewhat self-aware
   ☐ Not very self-aware
   ☐ Not self-aware

2. Currently, how aware are you of the unique design and gifts of those with whom you live, work, and serve?
   ☐ Very other-aware
   ☐ Somewhat other-aware
   ☐ Not very other-aware
   ☐ Not other-aware

3. Think of a time when one or more people complimented you for a skill or talent. Did you accept their words with gratitude, or did you discount their words because your actions didn't strike you as all that special? Based on what you discovered in this chapter, how, if at all, would your response change in the future?

# Chapter 5

# LOSING YOURSELF IN THE CYCLE OF FALSE IDENTITY

From 1989 to 1998 I was the director of New Life Ministries. In this Christ-centered program, participants drew on the twelve steps of recovery to help them deal with broken relationships within the safety of a small group. Before each participant was assigned to a group, he or she met with me. As a result, I had the privilege of hearing the life stories of thousands of people in relational crisis.

Just a few months after launching this ministry, I began to see repeating patterns of self-doubt, distrust, and frustration in the participants' lives. I later called the toxic relational system I had observed the Cycle of False Identity. This cycle was always triggered by significant persons (usually parents) who lacked self-awareness and then prevented their loved ones from recognizing their own unique gifts, makeup, and needs as well.

Even though most people are not very self-aware, they usually view themselves as pretty average. Sure, they may have a personality quirk or two, but who doesn't? Subconsciously they begin to view themselves almost as standards of normalcy. They tend to rate other people's weirdness or wrongness on a scale of how different these individuals are from themselves. Since they lack awareness of their own unique gifts and view themselves as standards of normalcy, they believe that if they can do something, just about everyone else should be able to do it too. It would be arrogant to think otherwise, right?

When I met Carol at New Life, I quickly realized that she had been caught in the Cycle of False Identity from an early age. Born into an upper-middle-class family in Omaha, she never lacked for material comforts. Her dad was a very successful executive for a multinational corporation. He was a kind man who loved his children, but he traveled frequently for business, often for weeks at a time. Like many men, her father formed his sense of identity through his work and his possessions.

Carol's mom was a tall, beautiful woman who had been a track star in both high school and college. After getting her degree, she continued her rigorous exercise regimen and participated in fund-raising runs, including marathons. Carol's mom brimmed with self-confidence and found her identity in her appearance and social standing.

Growing up, Carol did not seem to excel in anything. She grew into an attractive young woman, but she tended to be a little pudgy, no matter how much she exercised or dieted. Though her mother enrolled her in many different sports, Carol never found success there. Her older brother, on the other hand, was tall, good-looking, and very athletic. He was the apple of his mother's eye.

Carol seemed to be on the receiving end of a constant stream of criticism from her mother, who felt disappointed by her daughter's lack of athletic ability. Her father would cringe when he would hear his wife speak harshly to their daughter, but he seldom if ever intervened. In light of his frequent trips, the last thing he wanted to do when he was home was upset his wife. Unfortunately, in Carol's mind, his failure to stand up for her seemed to reinforce the "truth" of her mother's unmet expectations.

By the time Carol was a sophomore in high school, she had become obsessive about her weight and appearance. She often worked out on the treadmill for several hours a day and spent an excessive amount on new clothes. She had also become sexually active and was strangely drawn toward boys who treated her poorly. Now as a young woman in her midtwenties, Carol was in a dangerously abusive relationship. She did not feel she could go to her family for help. Carol had completely lost herself in the dynamics of her family and all of her mother's unfounded expectations.

Thankfully she was frightened enough by her situation to come to New Life. There she learned that her destructive behaviors were fueled by her unsuccessful attempts to try to be who her mother wanted her to be. Once she was given the freedom to be herself, Carol exhibited such a warm, witty personality and physical radiance that others were naturally drawn to her. She no longer shopped or exercised compulsively, because she was finally freed from trying to emulate her mother.

Carol's story illustrates how easy it is for a parent to have unrealistic expectations for his or her children. I do not believe that Carol's mother intended to harm her daughter. I am sure she believed that she had her daughter's best interests in mind whenever she communicated her disappointment.

I am not saying that all parental expectations are harmful either. In our home, one of the expectations my wife and I wholeheartedly agreed on was that all our children should exhibit gratitude. Always, without exception, our sons were taught to thank anyone who showed them any kindness or consideration. Showing good manners and respecting others are healthy, appropriate expectations.

However, there are good expectations and then there are unhealthy, unfounded assumptions, which too often are based on parents' own gifts, talents, and temperaments, as illustrated in Carol's story.

## THE CYCLE OF FALSE IDENTITY

The Cycle of False Identity, which devastates relationships, begins with a lack of self-awareness. When parents don't recognize their own giftedness, they tend to minimize it, dismissing it as nothing special. Then, because they see their talents as ordinary, parents project those gifts and talents onto their children. In other words, they expect their kids to demonstrate these same gifts and then judge them when they don't live up to the parents' unfounded expectations. Ultimately they may harshly label their children for failing to apply gifts and talents they do not possess. And the cycle generally repeats itself generation after generation.

*Because many parents see their own talents as ordinary, they expect their kids to demonstrate these same gifts and then judge them when they don't.*

✦  ✦  ✦

Let's take a closer look at each component within the cycle.

## Minimization

Most parents see themselves as pretty average—so normal, in fact, that they decide they are the "standard of normalcy." *Merriam-Webster's* defines *minimize* this way: "to reduce or keep to a minimum; to underestimate intentionally."[1] If your unique gifts and talents have not been recognized, affirmed, and celebrated—if the primary focus has been on what you lack rather than on what you possess—then it is very difficult not to minimize the gifts you do possess.

Another very powerful cause of minimization is false humility. Some people believe that any focus on one's own gifts and talents is somehow arrogant and self-centered.

Humility, they believe, requires them to act as if they have no gifts or strengths.

I find this belief to be present in many Christian environments, but it distorts the true meaning of humility. To deny your God-given gifts, talents, and intelligences is to deny His workmanship in your life. It's true that none of us have done anything to earn or deserve the blessings God has so lavishly poured out on each of us. Humility stems not from a denial of His good gifts but from a deep and profound sense of gratitude for all that He has done for us.

## Projection

Minimization almost inevitably leads to the phenomenon of projection, in which people falsely attribute their own gifts to others. If their abilities are nothing special, everyone should be able to do what they do, right? When Carol neither enjoyed nor excelled at swimming, tennis, or running—just three of the sports she tried—her mother assumed her daughter simply wasn't trying hard enough. Unfortunately, parents are typically as unaware of their children's gifts as they are of their own. Carol's mother was so disappointed at her daughter's lack of athletic abilities that she did nothing to nurture the gifts her daughter did have.

The psychological definition of projection has to do with the false attribution of feelings or characteristics, generally negative ones, to other people. I have found that people who are not very self-aware, who subconsciously minimize their unique set of gifts and talents, tend to subconsciously project or falsely attribute their own gifts and talents to other people as well.

Mike possesses a powerful internal drive and seemingly endless energy, which leads him to see his coworkers as lazy. Lydia has a gift for knowing exactly how others feel emotionally, but she is at a loss to understand why the women in her small group seem so insensitive to other people's feelings. Rob has a natural talent for organizing and creating order out of chaos but cannot understand why his wife seems so disorganized. These individuals all have unfounded expectations of others based on their own gifts, not on the talents of the individuals who are looking down the barrel of their "well-intended" assumptions.

*People who minimize their unique talents tend to subconsciously project or falsely attribute those same gifts to other individuals as well.*

✦   ✦   ✦

How many times have you said, "Oh, if I can do this, I know you can do it too." This is classic minimization and projection, and we have all done it. See if you recognize some of the thought patterns below, which reinforce our tendency to minimize and project.

*Commonality:* We have had the innate characteristics of our talents all our lives. Their development has typically been very gradual, almost imperceptible to us. Combine this with the common misunderstanding that all people are similar, and it is easy to see how we slip into thinking that our unique gifts and talents are common to most people. We may even act out of a false sense of humility; we do not want to see ourselves as better than anyone else.

*Familiarity and Comfort:* It just feels right to do it the way we do it because we are using our innate gifts and talents.

The converse feelings also reinforce minimization and projection, since areas in which we have no talent usually seem unfamiliar, uncomfortable, and ineffective. They "just don't look right" or "don't feel right." We typically assume these strengths are not only wrong for us, they are also flat-out wrong for anyone!

*Desire for Conformity:* At the very core of this mentality is the unconscious thought, *You need to be more like me.* It is the foundation from which we project our gifts and talents onto others: "This has always worked for me, so I know it will work for you if you will just try it." The exact opposite, that it feels uncomfortable and less efficient, is likely true for the person on the receiving end of the projection.

Let's consider a couple of examples of this kind of projection. I have worked with several couples where the husband and wife had very different preferences when it came to taking a vacation. The planners wanted to schedule every moment of the trip and tried to anticipate every possible contingency. The thought of being surprised or caught off guard during a trip unnerved them. These spouses had detailed checklists of every item needed for the trip. They knew exactly how many miles they would travel each day and where they would stop for breaks, meals, and lodging. They also knew how much each day would cost and where all the sightseeing options were. They often spent months planning every detail of the trip and thoroughly enjoyed the process, seeing it as a way to maximize the time and value of the vacation.

The planners' spouses were usually just the opposite. They loved the freedom, spontaneity, and sense of adventure that vacations provide. They thrived on surprises and the excitement of responding to unexpected challenges. Ideally, what they did on any given day of the vacation would depend on what they felt like doing on that day. Perhaps they would just want to sit by the pool, or maybe they would decide to go for a hike. "Can't know for sure until we get there" was their mantra. To their ultra-organized spouses, this was the height of irresponsibility and inefficiency. Not only that, it brought on stress. The adventurers, on the other hand, thought their spouses sucked all the fun out of their vacations and made them tedious, restrictive, and boring.

It's not just married couples who experience this type of frustration. I've also frequently seen teams of volunteer workers clash just after arriving at the site of their assignments, when the task-oriented volunteers square off against the people-oriented volunteers. Those intent on the task believe that, after a brief time for introductions, the focus should be on assigning and completing the work. Only after the project is finished should everyone be encouraged to sit around, have a beverage, and talk a bit. They are there to serve; meeting new people is not a priority or even a requirement.

People-oriented volunteers view that approach as simply rude. First, they want everyone to get to know each other over coffee and doughnuts. Then the group should decide who wants to work with whom. Such volunteers see their work as a relationship-building opportunity as well as a chance to serve.

In both examples, no one person is right or wrong; each person is simply demonstrating his or her own preference. Yet projection can become a significant relational issue. It even has the potential to lead to oppressive or abusive behavior when the one projecting is in a position of power over the one receiving the projection. Such situations can occur between parent and child, dominant and less dominant spouses, or boss and employee.

Once we have projected or falsely attributed our gifts and talents to another person, we also transfer the expectations we have for ourselves onto them. As an example, consider how this might have played out in my home. My wife and I set a very high standard in our family for reading books. My wife, Jaynee, was a history and English teacher, and she loves to read literature. From a young age, I loved reading a wide variety of nonfiction books. I even read the entire World Book Encyclopedia in my teens, which almost everyone else thought was just plain weird. Jaynee and I believe that reading books is of great value and a source of deep enjoyment.

As our sons were growing up, we implored them to read whenever possible. We read the Narnia series and other children's books to them when they were small. When they played baseball, we found books with stories about that sport. We tried rewarding them for reading; when that did not work, we implied that they were lazy and unmotivated. We told them that reading was the key to success in whatever field of study that they hoped to pursue.

> *Once we project our gifts onto another person, we also transfer the expectations we have for ourselves onto them.*
>
> ✦ ✦ ✦

We tried everything, but to no avail. None of our sons developed a love for reading! Oh, they read just fine when necessary, but they do not love it as we do. Our approach was a classic case of minimization and projection, since our love for reading is talent based and intrinsically motivated. No one told me to read the entire World Book Encyclopedia; I was intrinsically motivated to read it and thoroughly enjoyed the experience. No one told my wife to join a neighborhood literary book club; she was intrinsically motivated and looks forward to every meeting.

### Judging and Labeling

If Jaynee and I had then regarded our sons as flawed for not being avid readers, we would have been guilty of judging and labeling. We might have felt quite justified in our judgments, though our sons would have felt completely misunderstood and unfairly criticized.

Those who project out of their own lack of self-awareness attempt to find an explanation for the seemingly unexplainable behavior of others. After all, they are sure their children, employees, or friends could do what they do—if those people just tried harder, practiced longer, tried to be more sensitive, and so on.

Think back to the examples of vacationing spouses and volunteers. Quite likely, the planning husband or task-oriented volunteer thinks to himself, *Why does my wife [or fellow volunteer] lack common sense?* Yet for the woman who loves spontaneity and adventure, is it common sense to examine and plan every detail of the trip as her husband does? Is it common sense to a people-oriented volunteer to start work immediately without getting to know his teammates? The interesting thing is that most people seem to feel they have more than sufficient common sense and regularly use it.

*Merriam-Webster's* defines *common sense* as "sound and prudent judgment based on a simple perception of the situation or facts."[2] Considering how very differently people perceive reality, is there even such a thing as "simple perception"? No wonder common sense is anything but common.

Wikipedia says the term *common sense*, viewed in this way, "equates to the knowledge and experience which most people already have, or which the person using the term believes that they do or should have."[3] Ah, did you catch that? How do unique individuals come to "knowledge and experience" in common? This requires a high level of self-awareness, high awareness of others, and a good deal of dialogue.

Ralph Waldo Emerson said, "Common sense is as rare as genius—is the basis of genius." In my experience, common sense is that perception of reality and experience that works for individuals based on their unique set of gifts and talents. It feels obvious to the individuals because they perceive reality through the lens of their unique gifts, talents, and intelligences.

The key to breaking the Cycle of False Identity is understanding that we all see reality through our own unique lens. Without this self-awareness, we can conclude that other people lack common sense or are somehow defective, whether lazy, disorganized, or insensitive.

*Common sense is that perception of reality and experience that works for us based on our unique set of gifts and talents.*

✦ ✦ ✦

Eventually, such misjudgments become labels that people begin to apply to the individuals they are judging. As the labels stick, they discourage, disempower, and dehumanize, creating a crushing indictment against the judged individuals' sense of identity and worth. It becomes easy for those who judge to simply write off these individuals, deciding they no longer have to waste time trying to understand them. This judging and labeling feels very efficient and justified.

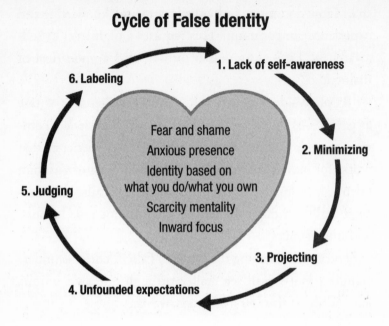

## Cycle of False Identity

1. Lack of self-awareness

2. Minimizing

3. Projecting

4. Unfounded expectations

5. Judging

6. Labeling

Fear and shame
Anxious presence
Identity based on
what you do/what you own
Scarcity mentality
Inward focus

## BREAKING THE CYCLE

The Cycle of False Identity is devastating to relationships, particularly because it tends to repeat itself from generation to generation. (See diagram above.) Parents who never gained self-awareness unconsciously project onto their children. Likewise, spouses project, friends project, and bosses project.

This cycle blocks people's gifts so they remain underdeveloped. In addition, people caught in it lose their true sense of identity, which means they no longer live authentic lives. Instead, they spend their lives trying to be who others expect them to be—people they are not and who God never intended them to be.

"An overemphasis on trying to overcome weaknesses creates much of the unhappiness in our world," says Dr. Caroline Leaf. "It is like trying to force the proverbial square peg into a round hole. It is the reason so many people seek but don't find meaning in their lives."[4] This leads to living a false identity, hiding one's true self behind a mask.

When people make significant life decisions based on false self-identity, potential disaster is not far away. Relationships do not work out as expected, nor do they seem to make sense. People feel generally misunderstood, which leads to an ever-present sense of fatigue and weariness. There is a pervasive lack of joy and a constant search for entertaining distractions. Fear becomes the primary motivator in life, especially fear of loss: loss of face, loss of relationships, loss of health, loss of resources, and loss of control. These fears can become self-fulfilling prophecies.

People caught in the Cycle of False Identity struggle with overwhelming fear. They begin to experience a host of toxic attitudes and thoughts, including anger, unforgiveness, self-pity, and jealousy. Research now shows that toxic thinking is lethal to our neurons, our brain cells. That's because toxic thinking produces a bath of chemicals in our brains that actually kills the cells there. Toxic thinking also suppresses our immune system, makes us physically sick and constantly tired, affects our ability to reason, and much more.

The Cycle of False Identity is pretty depressing, isn't it? Yet I believe there is an antidote. First, though, we have to look more deeply for the cycle's root. One of the first questions I asked people coming to New Life Ministries was, "What is the opposite of love?"

The most common response was "Hate." I would point out that this could not be correct, since God, who is pure love, hates many things, such as lies and the oppression and abuse of the weak. Then I would quote 1 John 4:18: "Such love has no fear, because perfect love expels all fear."

Fear is the opposite of love.

Perfect love, God's love, expels all fear.

Dr. Caroline Leaf describes just how incompatible love and fear are:

> The discovery that love and fear cannot coexist in our brains is revolutionary. In fact, scientists have researched the anatomy and physiology of love and fear right down to a molecular, genetic, and epigenetic level that can be described in detail.
>
> They have found a deeper system in the brain concerned with positive love emotions and negative fear emotions. They have discovered that these two systems cannot coexist, that at any one conscious moment, we will be operating in one or the other for each cluster of thoughts we think.[5]

So if people are constantly weighed down by fear, is there any hope that they can escape the cycle? Here is the exciting news:

Science is showing us that there is massive "unlearning" of negative toxic thoughts when we operate in love. The brain releases a chemical called oxytocin, which literally melts away the negative toxic thought clusters so that rewiring of new non-toxic circuits can happen. This chemical also flows when we trust and bond and reach out to others. Love literally wipes out fear![6]

Love wipes out fear. Can you see how powerfully people are affected when we communicate God's love to them through the blessing? The blessing can transform their lives. It can set them free to be who God has called them to be.

We were created in love and through love, intentionally and abundantly gifted for God's eternal purposes. We were created for interdependent relationships, to love and be a blessing to others so that they might know and praise the Father in heaven, the Creator of us all. In love, He has given each one of us blessings in the form of gifts, talents, and a calling. His blessings are so extravagant that if all people walked in their callings and contributed what God gave them to contribute, every need in our communities would likely be met.

APPLICATION ACTIVITY

After personally coaching over one thousand people, I think it is safe to say that almost every single person minimizes their gifts and talents. And nearly everyone has projected their gifts onto others at times.

1.  Growing up, did you experience any components of the Cycle of False Identity? Explain what that looked and felt like.

2.  As you think about how God has uniquely blessed you with gifts and talents, are there any ways in which you have minimized some aspect of your unique design?

3.  Specifically, which of your gifts and talents have you minimized?

4.  Can you recall times when you have projected any of your gifts or talents onto others? Describe one such instance.

5.  Are there people you may have unfairly judged, as if you assumed they possessed the same gifts and talents that you do?

6.  Is there anyone whom you have labeled and put in a
    box? I am not talking about people who are toxic and
    unsafe. We do need to set varying degrees of boundaries
    for such people. However, do certain people in your life
    bug you because you just don't "get them"? Explain.

*Chapter 6*

# ME, MYSELF, AND I:
# THE CONSEQUENCES
# OF FOCUSING ON SELF

While minimization, projection, judging, and labeling happen on an interpersonal level—between parent and child, teacher and student, or boss and employee—two cultural values also threaten our ability to give and receive the blessing: inflated self-esteem and radical individualism. Ironically, these two characteristics have been championed as means to affirm and strengthen people. As a result, their detrimental effects are often overlooked.

The blessing is not about high self-esteem, however. As we discovered in the last chapter, it's essential that parents understand that they have been uniquely designed—as have each of their children. When we live with that authentic identity, we gratefully recognize that there is something only *we* can do, even as we are thankful that people all around us are doing what only *they* can do.

Trying to bolster sagging self-esteem is no substitute for recognizing the gift God has put into each one of us. That leads to the realistic outlook that the apostle Paul advises we adopt: "Be honest in your estimate of yourselves, measuring your value by how much faith God has given you. . . . God has given each of us the ability to do certain things well" (Romans 12:3, 6, TLB).

Rather than valuing each person's abilities, our culture has wholeheartedly embraced high self-esteem; the evidence is everywhere. For example, imagine that you're sitting in the library of your local elementary school during a PTA meeting. Just after the treasurer gives the disappointing results from a recent major fund-raiser, talk turns to the school's upcoming field day. Each year the PTA underwrites the cost of this event, in which kids compete in a number of athletic competitions like the hockey shoot, obstacle course, and forty-yard dash.

Given the low balance in the PTA's checking account, the treasurer recommends that the group scale back its expenditures for this year's competition. Her suggestions that parents be asked to donate the juice boxes and granola bars and that the PTA forgo the cost of bringing in an inflatable obstacle course are met with nods all around the table. But then she makes a radical suggestion. What if the PTA no longer handed out medals to every student just for participating? The school could still award ribbons to the top three finishers in each event, she says, but the PTA would save several hundred dollars by dropping the participation medals.

The woman to your right frowns. She is thinking about her first-grade son, who is hopelessly uncoordinated but always cheerfully gives his best to everything. Doesn't he deserve a medal just for trying? The dad sitting across from you looks deep in thought too. His fifth-grade son loves to sprint and is a shoo-in for the blue ribbon in the forty-yard dash, but his sensitive third-grade daughter is sure to come home empty-handed and in tears if no participation medals are given out.

*Many kids never learn where they excel, both because they're not given meaningful incentives for real achievement and because they're encouraged to pattern themselves after someone else.*

✦ ✦ ✦

After these parents express their concerns, imagine someone turning to you and asking for your input. What would you say? While I don't have strong personal feelings about this scenario, I do find it ironic that we give every child a trophy so as not to damage his or her self-confidence, while at the same time we often expect that child to be just like us. As a result of these two conflicting approaches, many kids never learn where they excel, both because they're not given meaningful incentives for real achievement and because they're encouraged to pattern themselves after someone else.

## "LOOK AT ME!": THE TRAP OF INFLATED SELF-ESTEEM

"Confidence and satisfaction in oneself"—that's how my dictionary defines *self-esteem*.[1] Who could be opposed to that? I certainly agree that you and I should appreciate the high value and worth God has assigned to each one of us. So I'm not arguing that people shouldn't respect themselves and others. What I am suggesting is that we guard against inflated self-esteem.

The well-intended but misguided emphasis on high self-esteem in Western culture took hold in the twentieth century when researchers confirmed that low self-esteem can lead to antisocial and self-destructive behavior. As a way to counteract those issues, schools, youth sports programs, and the like began eliminating letter grades, distributing trophies to each player on the team, and awarding certificates to elementary students for just about everything. As this concept gained popularity, many people came to assume that high self-esteem closely correlates to well-being and psychological health.

However, not all parents and teachers have favored adopting self-esteem–building strategies at the cost of compromising kids' character and academic progress. In fact, they may be on to something. More recent research shows that nurturing high self-esteem does not produce the outcomes many had hoped—and in many cases even produces the opposite effect.

According to a 2006 study conducted by the Brown Center

on Education Policy at the Brookings Institution, although US eighth-graders had "only a middling performance" on an international math exam, they expressed high levels of confidence. They were also more likely to report that they "usually do well in mathematics" than were higher-performing students from countries like Singapore and South Korea.

Praise should be relevant to objective standards, said Chester E. Finn Jr., president of the Thomas B. Fordham Institute, an education think tank. Whether it's given to make children feel good or because they "at least tried," it's not helpful if students are still "50 yards from proficient," he said.

"Winning or losing also matters in the real world," Finn said. "You either beat the enemy or you don't. You either get the gold medal or you get the silver."[2]

Consider also this statement from Dr. Kristin D. Neff, an expert in human development:

Self-esteem does not appear to improve academic or job performance, to improve leadership skills, or to prevent children from smoking, drinking, taking drugs, and engaging in early sex. Bullies are as likely to have high self-esteem as others, and in fact, hassling other people and putting them down is one way that bullies feel good about themselves. People with high self-esteem are just as prejudiced if not more so than those who dislike themselves. They are also just as aggressive and engage in antisocial behavior like cheating, as often as people with low self-esteem do.[3]

As a case in point, social psychologist Jean M. Twenge explored the results of developing high self-esteem in the Millennial Generation (also known as Generation Y), generally considered to include those people born between 1981 and 1992. Many Millennials were exposed to this high self-esteem philosophy throughout their schooling.

In her book *Generation Me*, Twenge describes "two interlocking changes: the fall of social rules and the rise of the individual." According to Dr. Twenge, these two significant cultural changes dramatically affected how this generation was raised. This resulted in a general abandonment of basic rules of etiquette; a loss of respect for others, especially for elders; an almost epidemic use of profane language regardless of who might hear it; an acceptance of cheating, as long as no one gets caught; an obsession with appearance; an extension of adolescent behavior; materialism; and a casual view of sex.

Dr. Twenge uses the terms *internality* and *externality* to contrast healthy self-esteem with fragile high self-esteem. She says that those with internality, or healthy self-esteem,

- demonstrate good self-awareness of their personal attributes and understand that developing and applying them leads to accomplishment; and

- believe they have some degree of control over what happens to them.

On the other hand, externality, or fragile high self-esteem, leads people to believe that

- any failure in their lives, from being fired to failing a class, is the boss's or teacher's fault—it must be, since their artificially nurtured self-esteem assures them they know more than their superiors;
- social institutions should be viewed with cynicism; and
- outside sources, whether other people or luck, control their fate.

Twenge concludes,

> So here's how it looks: Generation Me has the highest self-esteem of any generation, but also the most depression. We are more free and equal, but also more cynical. We expect to follow our dreams, but are anxious about making that happen. In a recent poll, 53% of high school seniors said that growing up is harder now than it was for their parents.[4]

I frequently coach young people of this generation to help them uncover their strengths and map out their goals. In the process, I have discovered that many of their dreams are based more on their own expectations and wants than informed by the reality of who they are and what their authentic calling is. They tend to expect everything their parents had, plus a litany of personal wants: great house, nice cars, frequent travel, six-figure income, regular dinners out, maybe even their own business. I do not blame them for that; few young people have learned how to become self-aware or what will give them the greatest joy in their lives.

Not only can high self-esteem give people an inaccurate view of themselves, it can lead to a potentially dangerous egotism:

> Violence appears to be most commonly a result of threatened egotism—that is, highly favorable views of self that are disputed by some person or circumstance. Inflated, unstable, or tentative beliefs in the self's superiority may be most prone to encountering threats and hence to causing violence.[5]

The researchers who wrote the report above used a number of synonyms for high self-esteem, including *pride, egotism, arrogance, conceit, narcissism,* and *sense of superiority.* The authors end with this thought: "The higher (and especially the more inflated) the self-esteem, the greater the vulnerability to ego threats. Viewed in this light, the societal pursuit of high self-esteem for everyone may literally end up doing considerable harm."[6]

Some people associate the blessing with high self-esteem, assuming that we affirm the unique gifts in others so that they can feel better about themselves. I don't believe that is true. Unless people's sense of well-being comes from their understanding of their value and worth in God's eyes, they will always be vulnerable to the extremes of pride and insecurity.

## DOING MY OWN THING: THE DOWNSIDE OF INDIVIDUALISM

Closely linked to the blind pursuit of high self-esteem is the quest for expressive individualism. From the spouses who leave their marriages and families because they're unhappy or want to "find themselves" to the casual church hoppers who bounce from one congregation to the next, always seeking to find the church that meets all their needs, examples of the pursuit of a free and fulfilled self are all around us.

*Unless people's sense of well-being comes from their understanding of their value and worth in God's eyes, they will always be vulnerable to the extremes of pride and insecurity.*

✦ ✦ ✦

America has always seemed to have a love-hate relationship with the concept of individualism. Some see it as the primary source of many of our society's ills. In contrast, others see it as the foundation of our personal freedoms. In truth, individualism has always been central to the American way of life; however, its definition has evolved through the centuries. When inappropriately expressed, it, too, can prevent the blessing from being received and lived out.

*In the biblical tradition, individuals find their meaning, purpose, and identity as members of the Kingdom of God and their local faith community.*

✦ ✦ ✦

According to Robert N. Bellah et al., authors of *Habits of the Heart*, Western culture has embraced four traditions of individualism at various times. Two of the traditions, biblical and republican individualism, undergird our Declaration of Independence and Constitution. The other two, utilitarian and expressive individualism, emerged in the one hundred years following America's founding. Individualism rightly promotes "belief in the inherent dignity and, indeed, sacredness of the human person,"[7] but the four forms have some differences, as you'll see below:

### Biblical and Republican Individualism

*Similarity:* Both value the uniqueness of the individual while also seeing the individual in the context of community.

*Difference:* In the biblical tradition, individuals find their meaning, purpose, and identity as members of both the larger Kingdom of God and their local church. Republican[8] individualism encourages people to find their meaning and purpose within community and their civic contributions to that community.

*Early proponent of biblical individualism:* John Winthrop, who first described America as "a city upon a hill" and urged the Puritans to develop moral attributes.

*Early proponent of republican individualism:* Thomas Jefferson, who believed civic duty was the epitome of expression of moral freedom.

## Utilitarian and Expressive Individualism

*Similarity:* Both view the individual as primary; society is viewed as an artificial construct of secondary importance.

*Difference:* Utilitarian individualism sees people's relationship with society primarily through an economic lens, which arises from a theoretical contract that individuals enter to advance their self-interest. Expressive individualists believe it is paramount that each person seeks to uncover and express his or her unique core of feeling and intuition, generally without any regard for society as a whole.

*Early proponent of utilitarian individualism:* Benjamin Franklin, whose maxims and philosophy were so focused on individual self-improvement that the larger social context became less relevant to his followers.

*Early proponent of expressive individualism:* Walt Whitman, who reacted against the material self-interest that eventually became the focus of utilitarian individualism. He valued pursuing an experience-rich life, open to all kinds of people, and luxuriating in sensuality and in strong feelings.

Western individualism, expressed in these four distinct traditions, is a direct outcome of the various freedoms we are blessed to enjoy.

When nineteenth-century French political thinker Alexis de Tocqueville wrote about his travels throughout the United States, he said the young nation's key strength was not its favorable physical circumstances, which were plenty, but its laws and mores. These mores, or "habits of the heart," as he called them, were practices related to religion, political participation, and economic life. In other words, while Americans valued the worth of every individual, they were more committed to being good citizens and neighbors than to advancing their own interests. True freedom meant embracing attributes of character rather than seeking self-fulfillment.

*True freedom means embracing attributes of character rather than seeking self-fulfillment.*

✦ ✦ ✦

I believe that even today it is these core values, supported by our character traits and virtues, that distinguish healthy individualism from dysfunctional radical individualism. As the apostle Paul said, "You, my brothers and sisters, were called to be free. But do not use your freedom to indulge the flesh; rather, serve one another humbly in love" (Galatians 5:13, NIV).

Ultimately, expressive individualism leads to a self-centered focus on individual experience and sensuality. Expressive individualism can easily become a narcissistic existence without consideration of civic duty, Christian charity, or any sense of context other than a nebulous connection with nature and the universe as a whole.

Again, individualism is not the problem. In itself, it is not evil or self-centered. On the contrary, the Bible contains a rich heritage of individualism. Christian individualism recognizes each person's unique gifting and calling, which are based on the foundation of godly character and virtues. When expressed in mutual interdependence within the body of Christ, these gifts are essential for the spiritual health of the church as a whole.

Consider Galatians 5:22-23: "But the Holy Spirit produces this kind of fruit in our lives: love, joy, peace, patience, kindness, goodness, faithfulness, gentleness, and self-control. There is no law against these things!" As Christians, we are to exhibit the very character and virtues of God in our lives and especially in our interactions with other people. It is these virtues that utilitarian and expressive individualism generally lack.

## THE ATTITUDE OF GRATITUDE

Some may think the blessing is about high self-esteem and individualistic self-expression, but I have never seen that to be true. My observation is that those who receive the blessing first experience a profound sense of gratitude, which is then expressed to God and those they are in relationship with. This gratitude produces a deep humility and astonishment that God loves them and has so richly blessed them when they did nothing to deserve it.

There is no arrogance, egotism, or any sense of superiority; instead, there is a deep appreciation of others and their gifts. This appreciation grows into a genuine interest in other people. Then a compelling sense of responsibility to be faithful stewards leads them to use the blessings God has given them for the benefit of others. Grateful people understand Romans 12:4-5: "Just as there are many parts to our bodies, so it is with Christ's body. We are all parts of it, and it takes every one of us to make it complete, for we each have different work to do. So we belong to each other, and each needs all the others" (TLB).

Fortunately, millions of people in America and around the world are discovering that devoting all of their energies to advancing the self leads to a life that is shallow, unfulfilling, and lacking in meaning and purpose. An inflated self-esteem and radical individualism are dead ends when we are seeking to discover our meaning and purpose in life. These selfish pursuits ultimately lead to chronic loneliness.[9] Mutual interdependency—the very posture in which the blessing is given—leads to discovering who we truly are and using our gifts to benefit others.

APPLICATION ACTIVITY

There's a big difference between healthy self-esteem and inflated self-esteem. Responding to our gifts with joy and gratitude is appropriate. Viewing ourselves as entitled or superior to others, on the other hand, leads to a flimsy and fragile self-esteem, which is not based on reality.

Likewise, it is appropriate to affirm the dignity of every individual, including ourselves, which is a foundation of individualism. However, we must guard against the temptation to operate solely out of self-interest. To do so is to disregard God's intent when He gave us our gifts: to use them to benefit others.

1. Would you say your self-esteem is based on an accurate perception of your gifts and unique design, along with gratitude to your Creator? Or do you suspect it is based more on external factors like people's approval, your job title, or your financial portfolio?

2. Which expression(s) of individualism do you most identify with today? Explain.

3. Can you identify the primary expression of individualism displayed by your parents? Were they similar or dissimilar from each other? How about from you?

4. How would you say your parents' behavior helped form your views of individualism?

# Chapter 7

# A MATTER OF CHARACTER: WHY YOUR PARENTING STYLE MATTERS

Denise is concerned about her thirteen-year-old son, Stephen. Though she has never heard of the Cycle of False Identity, she is aware that her husband, Cal, has been putting unreasonable expectations on him. For instance, Cal doesn't understand why their son got a D on his last math test. Geometry always came easily to Cal, a mechanical engineer, and he is convinced Stephen is doing poorly in the class because he just isn't applying himself. Yesterday Cal spent an hour working with his son on spatial computations. Then he gave the boy a few problems to solve on his own while Cal went to their home office to check his e-mail.

Fifteen minutes later, Cal returned to their kitchen table and looked over his son's shoulder. He blew up when he saw that Stephen had filled his paper not with mathematical equations but with detailed pencil sketches of several characters from his favorite movie, *The Avengers*.

Rushing in from the laundry room, Denise tried to defuse the tension. "Stephen," she said, gently tousling his hair, "I know you had a long day at school today, but couldn't you have at least tried to do one of the problems?" Then without thinking, she complimented Stephen on the incredible detail in his drawings. Cal glared at her—though even he had admitted in the past that his son was an amazing artist.

"All right," Cal said. "I guess that's enough for today. But, Son, you must concentrate harder from now on in math class, got it?" As Stephen glumly nodded, Cal added, "Go wash your hands and set the table for Mom now."

Seeing her son's frown, Denise quickly said, "That's okay; I'll do it. I'll set the table and do the dishes for you tonight, Stephen, so you have some time to relax." She ignored her husband's startled look.

While Denise is correct in seeing that Cal's projection of his own math aptitude onto their son can be damaging, she is blind to the way in which she is failing to bless their son as well. By trying to compensate for her husband's "toughness," she is inadvertently coddling Stephen, which does nothing to strengthen his character.

Do virtue and character traits really matter when it comes to using and expressing our unique gifts and talents? I think so. Just consider whether you have ever known or heard of anyone who was immensely gifted and talented but whose life or career ended in disgrace and scandal because he or she lacked character. Without traits like wisdom, integrity, courage, love, justice, and temperance, our gifts and talents can never be used in the manner they were intended.

Gifts and talents are part of God's design for us; they are important indicators of our purpose. Each of us also has unique character strengths that powerfully affect our decisions, preferences, and behaviors. One way that we offer the blessing is calling out these strengths in other people, particularly our children.

Let me share an example. A beautiful little eleven-year-old girl I know recently had a painful encounter at her school. She is a sensitive child who shows strong empathy toward others and their feelings. She is also very accepting and aware of those who feel marginalized. In addition, she is responsible, well liked, and involved in many school activities.

*Without traits like wisdom, integrity, courage, love, justice, and temperance, our gifts and talents can never be used in the manner they were intended.*

✦ ✦ ✦

One day she overheard a group of "in" girls, some of whom were close friends of hers, bullying and verbally deriding a shy, not very popular girl. This courageous eleven-year-old stepped between the group and the shy girl. She then confronted the group for its hurtful behavior, demonstrating bravery and integrity, two character strengths. She paid a high price for this act of courage. It cost her several friendships within the group, and she herself was verbally attacked for weeks, which caused her great emotional pain.

But given the opportunity, she would have done the very same thing again. This provided a wonderful opportunity for her parents to recognize, celebrate, and reinforce her virtues and character strengths.

Even in the midst of incredible diversity among people, there are core, unchanging moral values that are universally treasured across time and cultures. "Certain moral values," writes Sissela Bok, "go to the heart of what it means to be human and always have, since the beginning of time, and always must if we are not to lose touch with our humanity."[1]

*Even in the midst of incredible diversity among people, there are core, unchanging moral values that are universally treasured across time and cultures.*

✦ ✦ ✦

Character strengths enable us to make right, moral decisions in our thoughts, words, and actions, toward both ourselves and others. One could say that how we use our gifts and talents is determined by our character strengths and virtues. Likewise, the more you and I develop and express these character traits, the more readily we will be able to bless others. Character sets us free to recognize and celebrate others even though they may be very different from ourselves. The VIA Institute on Character has done extensive global research on character strengths and virtues, and we'll look more closely at recognizing and cultivating those specific traits in part 3.

How are character strengths developed? Once again, parents play a key role. Researchers have identified three parenting styles, each of which has a powerful influence—positive or negative—on the development of children's character.

## PERMISSIVE PARENTING

Denise is a classic example of a permissive parent, who *focuses on the wants of the child and the wants of the parent* while ignoring the essential needs of the child. Like Denise, permissive parents appear to be warm and loving. They typically do not want to experience the conflict and hard work of setting rules and standards and then enforcing them. This frequently leads them to offer bribes and promises to get their children to comply with their wishes.

One problem with parents focusing on the wants of their children is that these desires are, in fact, insatiable. Parents who try to meet their child's every want produce children who may become narcissistic with inflated egos. Feeding into this is the permissive parents' inclination to think the best of their children, which may lead them to rationalize and excuse their children's inappropriate behavior.

*Children of permissive parents frequently become self-absorbed adults who have never learned to delay gratification or put the interests of others ahead of their own.*

✦ ✦ ✦

Permissive parents fail to set consistent boundaries for their children; as a result, children of permissive parents frequently become self-absorbed adults who have never learned to delay gratification or put the interests of others ahead of their own.

These parents want to bless their children. The problem is that they tend to try to bless their children through materialism and freedom without the required character development and responsibility. Ironically, children of permissive parents may begin to interpret the absence of set boundaries and standards as a lack of caring by their parents and can become resentful. This approach serves only to confuse the children concerning their authentic identity.

Leadership consultant James C. Hunter describes it particularly well:

> I observe far too many parents attempting to be "best buddy" to their children by running around trying to gratify their never-ending wants rather than providing the leadership they need. Leadership that provides boundaries, love, feedback, and discipline that children so desperately *need* to be the best they can be. I see parents more concerned with spoiling and lavishing upon their children the material things they themselves did *not* receive growing up while failing to provide them with the important things they *did* receive from their parents.[2]

A variation of permissive parenting is the uninvolved parent, who focuses only on his or her own needs. Uninvolved parents also refuse to impose rules and standards; they believe the kids will regulate themselves. Yet uninvolved parents are absent emotionally and oftentimes physically. To the child, this feels like abandonment.

I remember one night when I was a freshman in high school and I came home with a black eye. When my father asked how I got it, I explained that a teacher had punched me in the face during class.

His response was quite matter-of-fact: "I am sure you deserved it." That was the end of the discussion.

My father had never attended a parent-teacher conference; he had no idea what was happening at school other than what he picked up by reviewing my report cards. He didn't attend a single one of my athletic events or any of my activities in Boy Scouts. What my siblings or I did in those venues was of no concern to him as long as it did not bring him negative attention. He was modeling the same style of parenting that he had experienced.

## AUTHORITARIAN PARENTING

This style of parenting is driven by a *focus on the wants and needs of the parent* while ignoring the essential needs of the child. The authoritarian parent's primary goal is to control others, which leads to an undercurrent of distrust.

Like most authoritarian parents, Cal holds his son, Stephen, to high standards, some of which are quite appropriate. In the process, the children of authoritarian parents often learn the value of hard work and self-discipline. The problem comes when these parents believe that without their constant vigil, their children will not do what they should. Such moms and dads often appear cold, distant, and unapproachable. They use such psychological tactics as anger, shaming, withdrawal of love, and threats to enforce their control. Seldom do they see any reason to explain their demands, yet they view any delay in compliance or any questioning as acts of disobedience that must be punished.

Generally such parents believe their children are blank slates on which they, as responsible parents, need to write everything the children should be. Authoritarian parents tend to be moralistic perfectionists; as a result, their children begin to believe they will never be good enough, obedient enough, smart enough, or hardworking enough. In short, such children may conclude that they are defective and irreparably broken, and their character development will likely be stunted.

*The consequences of authoritarian parenting are sobering: it often produces wounded, angry, and resentful children.*

✦ ✦ ✦

The consequences of authoritarian parenting are sobering: it often produces wounded, angry, and resentful children. Researchers studying kindergartners showed that shaming these children for poor performance led them to perform more poorly on problem-solving tasks. Other research shows that people, particularly children, learn better from positive feedback than they do from negative feedback.[3]

Children coming from authoritarian homes feel less socially accepted than their peers and are less resourceful as well. It might seem logical, however, that authoritarian parenting would at least lead to higher rates of morality. However, research has disproved this: "Authoritarian parents might see themselves as champions of morality. But . . . studies suggest that kids with authoritarian parents are actually *less* advanced when it comes to moral reasoning."[4]

## THE WORST OF BOTH WORLDS

Often when one parent's primary parenting style is authoritarian, the other will play the role of a permissive parent in an attempt to provide balance. In this case, the children receive the disadvantages of both styles, causing profound confusion in the children and often deep resentment between the two parents. Unfortunately, this is where Stephen is trapped.

This was true in my home growing up as well. My father seemed to function in two extremes. Depending on the context, he was either authoritarian or uninvolved. Whenever we were in his presence, he was authoritarian. Yet he never attended anything we were involved with at school or church.

Later in life he reverted more frequently to the uninvolved parenting style, whether he was at work, at the bar, or off on a fishing or hunting trip. However, whenever he was present—which was seldom—he functioned in the authoritarian parenting style. My mother acted more as a classic permissive parent. To a great degree, I believe she did this to try to counteract the harshness of my dad's authoritarian style. It was a very confusing environment.

A common outcome of both authoritarian and permissive parenting is an unhealthy codependency between parent and child. For instance, I tried desperately to win my father's approval; in fact, my sense of identity was tied to whether or not I succeeded. The more I needed his approval, the more he backed away and withheld it from me. Looking back, I suspect my need threatened him because he felt he had nothing to offer me.

This type of codependency affects both parent and child in that both tend to derive their sense of identity from the other's behavior. This then reinforces the efforts and manipulation of each to get the other to behave in the desired way. Children may have the foreboding sense that they have lost control of their lives and cannot trust anyone. They then desperately attempt to regain that control by trying to control others.

Trust provides the foundation for maturity, yet both authoritarian and permissive parents fail to foster an environment where trust can grow. That's why Stephen is likely to end up resenting both his parents. Even now he doesn't feel very close to Cal, nor does he really trust him. Stephen is already convinced he'll never live up to his dad's expectations. Though he has warmer feelings toward his mom, with time he is likely to resent the fact that she never had the courage to stand up to his dad—or to hold Stephen to appropriate expectations for himself.

## AUTHORITATIVE PARENTING

Unlike *authoritarian* moms and dads, *authoritative* parents strike the right balance *by focusing on the essential needs of the child and the needs of the parents.* They set clear boundaries, high standards, and appropriate consequences. They explain the reasons for all three to their children.

Authoritative parents encourage their children to ask questions, which helps children not only to comply but also to internalize values and character traits. Authoritative parents respect their children as unique persons in the process of becoming mature and responsible people. They understand the importance of identifying their children's intrinsic motivations and feelings. Authoritative parents expect cooperation and mutual respect from their kids, even as they are emotionally and physically available to them.

*Authoritative parents respect their children as unique persons in the process of becoming mature and responsible people.*

✦ ✦ ✦

There is growing evidence that children of authoritative homes look to their parents rather than their peers when making important decisions. These kids are viewed as more helpful and kind—and therefore are often more popular—than their classmates. Finally, because they have learned "inductive discipline" from parents who explain the reasons for their rules, such children demonstrate more advanced moral reasoning skills than other children do.[5]

In the book of Ephesians, the apostle Paul contrasts

permissive and authoritarian parenting with authoritative parenting:

> *Fathers, do not irritate and provoke your children*
> *to anger [do not exasperate them to resentment],*
> *but rear them [tenderly] in the training and disci-*
> *pline and the counsel and admonition of the Lord.*
> (Ephesians 6:4, AMP)

How do parents exasperate their kids? By trying to en-force limits that are too controlling—or by neglecting to establish many limits at all. After cautioning parents against provoking their children, the apostle Paul perfectly sums up the essence of authoritative parents, who "rear them [tenderly] in the training *and* discipline and the counsel *and* admonition of the Lord" (emphasis mine). In other words, it's not enough to set high standards; parents must also be responsive to their children's needs. Likewise, it's not enough to be sensitive to children's feelings; moms and dads must set appropriate expectations.

| SUMMARY OF PARENTING STYLES | | |
|---|---|---|
| | **Expectations** | **Responsiveness** |
| **Permissive** | Low | High |
| **Authoritarian** | High | Low |
| **Uninvolved** | Low | Low |
| **Authoritative** | High | High |

## THE LIES WE BELIEVE

These styles not only affect the way parents treat their children, they also determine the myths children pick up. In permissive homes, children are often told, "If you can dream it, you can do it." I refer to this lie as the *American Idol* Syndrome.

My wife loves to watch *American Idol*, so I've seen quite a few episodes myself. In the early phase of each season, we are subjected to what seems like an endless number of performances by individuals who are just awful! I often feel sorry for these people, since the program seems to exploit and expose their folly to the world. However, something became very apparent to me early on; most of these performers actually believe they can sing. Despite their confidence, they lack the major component necessary to success—talent!

How can individuals be so delusional? I suspect it's because many of their parents, though well meaning, falsely proclaimed that their kids could do anything they wanted to do. Some parents, not wanting to dash their children's dreams, even go so far as to lie about how much innate talent they see in their children.

When I first watched the program, I found only one thing more startling than the horrible singing voices of these worst performers: their reaction when judge Simon Cowell told them that they were awful and that their voices were like razor blades to the eardrum. Some performers exploded in anger, some cursed him, some told him he was an idiot, and some even fell to their knees, begging for one more chance as they cried, "But this is my dream!"

Of course, that is the problem—a dream undertaken without the necessary talent is just a pipe dream. Accepting that truth and reality is a blessing; affirming that which is not true can become a curse.

The myth that is much more prevalent in authoritarian homes is, "You can be anything that you want to be [or that I want you to be] if you just try hard enough." The inference in this belief is that children must not only become competent in an area outside their comfort zone, they must excel in it. This one may sound more realistic than "If you can dream it . . . ," but actually it is just as misleading.

Anytime I did not excel in a particular endeavor, my dad's response was, "You are just not trying hard enough. You have to try harder!" This was especially true in areas for which I clearly lacked the necessary talent. The only things his counsel produced in my life were frustration, a sense of failure, and the belief that I was defective.

When trying to advance this "just try harder" myth, some people quote from the famous speech Winston Churchill gave to his old preparatory school in 1941: "Never give in. Never give in. Never, never, never, never—in nothing, great or small, large or petty—never give in except to convictions of honor and good sense. Never yield to force; never yield to the apparently overwhelming might of the enemy."

Churchill, however, was not talking about persisting at something you were never designed to do. The key to understanding Churchill's statement comes from considering the timing of this speech. If an enemy is threatening to bomb and obliterate you from the face of the earth, as was the case in England during World War II, "never give in" is good advice. However, if this counsel is applied to an area of life in which you lack the talent to accomplish the goal, it is very bad advice. For example, if individuals with no singing talent practice every day, will they be successful? No. In reality, they will have wasted their time trying to be something they were never intended to be.

In the end, parenting styles play a huge role in whether or not moms and dads speak the language of blessing in the lives of their children. The two myths we just discussed, for instance, are both major sources of misinformation. They make it much harder for young people to discover their true calling in life. These myths discourage and confuse young people while taking their attention away from developing their authentic gifts, talents, and character strengths.

While it's helpful to understand the differences between the three parenting styles, most parents fall somewhere on the continuum between permissive, uninvolved, and authoritarian. However, vacillating between authoritarian and permissive does not equal out to authoritative parenting, in the same way that having an authoritarian parent and a permissive parent does not equal an authoritative home.

Families sometimes do not fit neatly within these classifications. In addition, there is often movement along the continuum during the various seasons of family life. I have heard many firstborn children tell me they felt as if their parents were rather authoritarian while raising them, only to adopt a more permissive parenting style with a younger sibling.

What if your parents never learned to speak the language of blessing? How about the supervisor who never affirms you today? Remember that the blessing does not originate with our parents or any other person—it originates with God. God's original plan was for your parents to be the first to give you His blessing, but too often it does not work out that way. Yet God is persistent in His desire to bless you even through those who are not your parents, if you will just be open to receive that blessing.

APPLICATION ACTIVITY

Children raised by authoritarian parents are constantly told, "You'd be able to do that if you just tried harder," while children raised in permissive homes get the message, "You can do anything you want in life." Both directives make it more difficult for children to find their true calling, since they don't encourage the discovery and development of a child's authentic gifts, talents, and intelligences.

1. What was the primary parenting style that you experienced as a child?

2. Did your parents use similar or dissimilar parenting styles?

3. How did that affect your view of each of your parents?

4. How has this affected you as an adult?

5. If you are a parent, what is your primary style of parenting? What is your spouse's? What effect has your parenting style had on your ability to speak the language of blessing?

*Part 3*

# LEARNING
# TO SPEAK
# THE LANGUAGE
# OF BLESSING

# Chapter 8

# KNOW YOURSELF:
# BECOMING SELF-AWARE

Walking into the large sanctuary of a church several years ago, I was greeted almost immediately by Nora, who moved toward me with such a warm and welcoming smile that I instantly felt comfortable. I had flown from my home in Nebraska to New York to conduct leadership training for the staff at her church.

If I hadn't been convinced that Nora was leading out of her strengths simply by the way she welcomed me, any doubts vanished a few moments later. After we had exchanged brief greetings, Nora told me she would be taking me to the church office to meet the rest of the staff. Just then the door at the back of the church opened, and I saw someone shuffle into the sanctuary. Very quickly the woman sat down in a pew near the back of the church and put her head in her hands.

Nora touched me softly on the shoulder and, looking back at the woman, said, "I hate to do this to you, Joe, but I need to speak to that person. Excuse me just a minute."

She walked back to the pew and sat down beside the visitor. As the two of them spoke together in low tones, Nora put an arm around the woman. It was obvious that Nora was consoling her in some way.

About fifteen minutes later, Nora walked the woman to the back door and saw her out before returning to my side. She apologized again for having to excuse herself.

"No problem," I said. "I assume you were talking to one of your parishioners."

"No," Nora said.

"Oh, so it's someone from the community you've been working with?"

Nora shook her head. "Joe, I've never seen that woman before."

"Really?" I asked. "Well, then how did you know how to approach her?"

"I just knew," Nora said, "that she needed someone to comfort her right now."

It was obvious to me that Nora was wired to be empathetic; in fact, when I met with the church staff later to discuss their leadership strengths, Nora confirmed that Empathy was the number one talent that emerged when she took an assessment called StrengthsFinder, which we'll talk more about later in this chapter.

I love watching people lead with their talents, so I was

surprised when Nora told me her reaction when she first received the assessment results: "I was with the other staff members, and I was mortified to see Empathy listed as my top talent. 'That's not a strength!' I said. 'That's a weakness.'"

Nora, I learned, had just one brother who was a number of years older than she was. From the time she was three or four, Nora remembers her brother and father regularly getting into heated discussions. As they argued, their voices got louder and louder. Scared, Nora would begin to cry, drawing her dad's attention.

Rather than trying to comfort her, her father would order her to be quiet. "Stop acting like a baby, Nora. Your brother and I are just talking."

The message Nora took away? Showing emotions is bad. So she tried to squelch her tears, as well as her tendency to reach out to others. Inadvertently, her father had deprived her of the blessing she craved from him—not only did he never affirm her warm, encouraging spirit, she actually felt demeaned for having it.

As a natural empathizer, Nora had both an intrinsic need for empathy and a need to express her feelings. Yet because her dad had convinced her that people shouldn't show emotions, she repressed her talent as if it were actually a weakness. Fortunately, once she expressed her dismay over her talent to her coworkers, they came around her and told her they'd seen this strength in her and affirmed her for it. In that moment, she was released to be herself. Until her giftedness had been acknowledged, it wasn't real to her. Now she is flourishing as she expresses her gift of empathy with a new sense of purpose and freedom.

*Until your giftedness has been acknowledged, it isn't real to you.*

✦ ✦ ✦

In chapter 2, I explained that you, along with every other human being, were created with a unique genius—a one-of-a-kind blend of personality, talents, intelligence, and character. The blessing is God's way of affirming those gifts within you. Ideally, your parents were the first ones to recognize those gifts and speak the language of blessing. Quite likely, though, they themselves never received the blessing and were caught in the Cycle of False Identity, which prevented them from calling out their own gifts, let alone yours.

Nora's church has made it a priority to help its members discover their strengths. Since empathy comes naturally to Nora, her role in her church now is to help others discover and begin expressing their spiritual gifts and talents.

Whether or not you have received words of blessing from your parents or church community, you can discover how you've been gifted, thanks to a number of proven assessments that are widely available. If you're like many of the people I coach, you may fear that if you take an assessment, it will only reveal your weaknesses or even prove you have no gifts. It may also seem like a cold and clinical process. In reality, I have found the opposite to be true. By revealing your preferences and strengths (which everyone has), these tools provide natural opportunities to talk with others, such as family members or a small faith-group community, about your talents, calling, and purpose. It's an environment in which the language of blessing can be spoken and received. When this happens, the blessing is activated within you.

*Assessments provide natural opportunities to talk about your talents, calling, and purpose.*

✦ ✦ ✦

If you are unconvinced that God created you with a special purpose or are not sure of your strengths, I encourage you to learn how any or all of the assessments below can help you determine your unique genius.

## YOUR TALENTS

If you say someone has a talent, many people immediately assume you're talking about that person excelling in an ability like singing or playing football. When I speak of talents, however, I'm drawing on the work of Dr. Don Clifton[1] and his team at Selection Research Inc., which set out over forty years ago to investigate what distinguishes the best performers in any given role. Their conclusion? The highest achievers in the workplace or the classroom all focus on their talents—"any recurring pattern of thought, feeling, or behavior that can be productively applied."[2]

On the one hand, that sounds obvious. Don't we all do best where we're naturally gifted? But initially Clifton's research was revolutionary. If you think about it, our parents, teachers, coaches, and employers often seem to emphasize the areas where we need to improve. Nora learned to repress her natural empathy because her father did not value it. Something similar might happen to a salesman who is relational and likes variety in his work but whose boss is structured and disciplined. When the employee's annual review comes around, his supervisor may tell him he needs to spend less time chatting with clients and more time completing reports. By focusing on this "weakness" to the exclusion of the employee's many strengths, this supervisor leaves the employee feeling demoralized. Not only has this boss disregarded the value of the salesman's people skills, but he expects the employee to set aside his preferences to behave in a way that seems more natural to his boss.

Nearly twenty years after Clifton founded Selection Research Inc., it had grown into a large human resources consulting company. In 1988, SRI acquired the Gallup Organization. Over the following decade, Gallup continued to study human strengths. Eventually, after interviewing 1.7 million people, researchers identified numerous human talents that could be productively applied in any organization. They then grouped them into thirty-four talent themes. Gallup later developed the Clifton StrengthsFinder assessment as a helpful tool people could use to identify their own talents and gifts.

Clifton pointed out that a talent and a strength are not synonymous. A person must invest time into gaining knowledge, skill, and experience related to the talent so that it develops into a strength. In their bestselling book *Now, Discover Your Strengths*, Marcus Buckingham and Clifton profiled several individuals at the top of their fields, explaining how each of them "had identified in themselves some recurring patterns of behavior and then figured out a way to develop these patterns into genuine and productive strengths."[3] The book also included a code readers could use to access the StrengthsFinder assessment, which enabled readers to determine their top five talents as well. (Today the code is also available in the books *How Full Is Your Bucket?*, *Living Your Strengths*, *StrengthsFinder 2.0*, *StrengthsQuest*, and *Strengths-Based Leadership*.[4] The assessment can also be accessed directly at www.gallupstrengthscenter.com.)

Dr. Chip Anderson was a close friend of Don Clifton. While working with remedial students at UCLA, he realized he didn't just want to see his students pass courses—he wanted to see them thrive. He then spent years creating a Strengths Revolution on high school and college campuses, which spread to more than four hundred educational institutions. Shortly before his death in 2005, Anderson reflected on the genius he saw in each of the thirty-four talents in a paper he presented to the board of trustees at Azusa Pacific University, where he was a professor:

From my experience, each of the themes of talent identified by the Clifton StrengthsFinder Inventory has a stroke of genius within it. The genius of our talents reflects what those talents enable and empower us to do to potential levels of excellence. The concept of genius refers to an extraordinary ability to do certain things, and as such there is great beauty in seeing what is done by the genius within individuals.[5]

Whenever I coach people who missed out on the blessing from their parents, I witness the incredible sense of affirmation they get from taking StrengthsFinder and beginning to understand the purpose for which they were created.

There is a temptation to see certain talents as more important than others, but that is a mistake. Every gift and talent is equally valuable and important. Every combination is uniquely valuable as well. Incredibly, the same top five talent themes occur only once in every 275,000 people. If the order of those five themes is factored in, the profile occurs an average of once in 33.4 million people. The figure drops to one in approximately 447 trillion people who have the identical top ten talent themes in the same order of strength.

Your gifts and talents are tools for you to use to fulfill your calling in life. We are compelled, intrinsically motivated, to function in our God-given talents. While no one talent is more valuable than another, each needs to be developed properly and used appropriately. I like to compare our top talents to a team of horses. They are powerful, and we are driven to express them, to let them "run." Unless we understand why we do what we do, however, that can lead to problems.

Suppose you are a highly empathetic person serving on a committee that awards grants. If a fellow committee member values responsibility and achievement most highly, he may recommend turning down a proposal from a worthy organization simply because it varies a bit from your grant guidelines. If you feel compassion for the organization, you may decide he's being hard-hearted and inflexible. But if you push back on his recommendation, he may accuse you of being too sentimental and lax. That is why self-awareness is so important. We have to be aware, both of what our preferences and strengths are and of the fact that God has given us "reins" to pull back our talents at the appropriate times so they do not drive every response and decision we make.

You can use your reins—your self-awareness—to emphasize, focus, or restrain a certain talent when that is most appropriate. Each of your talents was given to you to be used in the appropriate way and at the appropriate time. The more self-aware you become, the more you will learn to use them expertly.

## YOUR CHARACTER

Talents are great—but are they everything?

I often ask people, "What happens if someone has developed his or her talents and intelligences to a great extent, but this person lacks character and virtue?"

The most common response to that question? "You get a Hitler."

I am surprised at how universally people understand that great talent and intelligence without character and virtue is potentially a very dangerous combination.

We have seen incredibly talented and highly intelligent individuals give us debacles like Enron, the financial collapse of 2008, and a seemingly endless parade of moral failings—all of which have resulted in great harm. God's dream and plan is that every individual will use his or her unique gifts to bless others. The very nature of the blessing, then, is that it is to be used for the good of both the individual and the community.

That's why I am deeply saddened whenever I see the transformational power of a person's calling distorted into something selfish, often nothing more than an attempt to satisfy that individual's own exaggerated wants. Recognizing and developing character and virtue is essential to preventing that from happening.

Psychologist Martin Seligman is considered one of the founders of "positive psychology," which focuses on the empirical study of positive emotions and strength-based character. Collaborating with fellow psychologist Christopher Peterson, Seligman created the VIA (Values in Action) Inventory of Strengths Survey, a questionnaire designed to help people identify their character strengths—those attributes that are universally understood to be essential to a satisfying and meaningful life.

After examining core characteristics valued by both moral philosophers and religious thinkers through the ages, the researchers agreed on six virtues: wisdom and knowledge, courage, humanity, justice, temperance, and transcendence.

They then identified a total of twenty-four character strengths—characteristics through which one of the six virtues is expressed:

*Wisdom and knowledge:* creativity, curiosity, open-mindedness, love of learning, and perspective

*Courage:* bravery, persistence, integrity, and zest

*Humanity:* love, kindness, and social intelligence

*Justice:* citizenship, fairness, and leadership

*Temperance:* forgiveness and mercy, humility/modesty, prudence, and self-regulation

*Transcendence:* appreciation of beauty and excellence, gratitude, hope, humor, and spirituality

Seligman and his team developed the VIA survey as a tool to help users learn to apply their character strengths to their daily responsibilities and relationships so they could live out their potential with greater satisfaction while contributing to the good of society.[6]

Each of us has a unique set of character traits and virtues. Our signature character traits come more easily to us and tend to form our most cherished core values. It is important to note that just because a character trait is low in our report does not mean that we lack that character trait. It does mean we must be much more intentional in expressing that particular character trait in our lives.

I once coached Emily, a young woman whose father was a judge and whose mother was a high school principal. Both were highly responsible, driven people. Emily was a college sophomore who was failing several of her classes. She'd also recently been arrested for driving under the influence. During one of our first meetings, she insisted that she had no character strengths—unlike her parents, who were respected throughout their community.

Nonetheless, Emily agreed to take the VIA Character Strengths Survey, which revealed that her top character strengths are appreciation of beauty and excellence, citizenship, social intelligence, zest, and bravery. As I talked with her, I discovered she felt most alive whenever she was surrounded by nature. She also loved to work with the elderly and was valued for her loyalty and kindness by her many friends. Furthermore, even though she felt looked down on by the adults in her life for not being more responsible and self-controlled, she refused to judge them in return. As I pointed out her many character qualities, she was finally empowered to value and nurture them.

Overall, I have found that once individuals identify and develop their innate virtues and character traits, it's much easier for them to focus on developing the others. You may also find it helpful, as I have, to spend time with friends who have your lower character traits among their signature traits. Because I love and respect these friends, I can also admire and learn more about how they live out these particular character traits in their lives.

There is no charge to take this character assessment or to receive the results. There is also a VIA Character Strengths Survey for Children and another for youth. Both are free. As of this writing, you can take your Character Strengths Survey at www.viacharacter.org.

*Once individuals identify and develop their innate virtues and character traits, it's much easier for them to focus on developing the others.*

✦ ✦ ✦

## YOUR PERSONALITY

Why do you respond differently than your family members, coworkers, or friends to some of the same events? The Myers-Briggs assessment seeks to explain this by determining the way each person perceives other people, things, and situations, as well as how he or she makes decisions. Developed by Katharine Cook Briggs and her daughter, Isabel Briggs Myers, this personality inventory was created to help women entering the industrial workforce during World War II find jobs that would provide the best fit for them. The Myers-Briggs Type Indicator was first published in 1962. The ninety-three-question assessment is designed to determine the users' preferences in four different areas:

*Extraversion or introversion:* Do they draw energy from and prefer to concentrate on the outer world (E—extraversion) or their inner world (I—introversion)?

*Sensing or intuition:* Do they prefer to gather information from what they take in through their senses (S—sensing), or do they prefer to assign meaning to that data (N—intuition)?

*Thinking or feeling:* Do they prefer to make decisions based on logic (T—thinking), or do they prefer to consider other people and extenuating factors (F—feeling)?

*Judging or perceiving:* In their interactions with the outside world, do they prefer to come to a final decision (J—judging), or do they prefer to remain open to new data and opportunities (P—perceiving)?

In all, there are sixteen distinctive personality types, which result from the possible combinations of these four preferences (e.g., ISTJ, ESTJ, INTJ, ENTJ, etc.). No one type is better than another, so there is no wrong way to see the world, only different ways. I am a highly extraverted, intuitive, thinking, and perceiving person. As a result, spending time with people energizes me, and I love being part of a team. I naturally bring many ideas and a great deal of creativity to projects. I do not enjoy routine or doing things the way they have always been done. I love concepts as long as I see how they can be applied, and I frequently let ideas brew for extended periods of time. As a result, progress on my projects tends to be somewhat sporadic, and I often struggle to complete them all unless I can work on them with a team.

How can a personality assessment help provide the blessing you long for? Perhaps you grew up in the shadow of a popular and social older brother. At the beginning of the school year, your teacher had high expectations that you, too, would be a class leader simply because your brother was always the first with his hand up and often enlivened class with witty banter.

At the start of every school year, you detected a look of disappointment when that same teacher asked you a question and you froze. You were no less intelligent than your brother; you simply needed time to process and consider new information. In fact, because you took extra time to consider data, your conclusions often had greater depth than your brother's—problem is, your teacher never followed up with you after you had internalized and processed new information.

More than likely, the Myers-Briggs Type Indicator would show that you have a preference for introversion, whereas your brother appears to prefer extraversion. Neither is better than the other, but your preference affects how you take in information and interact with your world. (For more information on the various types and their impact on relationships, as well as how to take the assessment from a qualified professional, visit www.myersbriggs.org.)

## YOUR INTELLIGENCE

When it comes to understanding your intelligence, the question is not, "How intelligent are you?" but "How are you intelligent?" That's because scientists and educators now know there are multiple types of intelligence. This understanding is relatively new and revolutionary.

Before 1983, there was one primary understanding of intelligence and one tool to measure it: the psychometric IQ test. An IQ of 100 showed average intelligence, while anyone with an IQ over 140 was considered a genius.

That simplistic understanding was expanded in 1983, when Howard Gardner, a professor of cognition and education at Harvard, published *Frames of Mind: The Theory of Multiple Intelligences*. Until recently, Gardner noted,

> It was generally believed that intelligence was a single entity that was inherited, and that human beings—initially a blank slate—could be trained to learn anything, provided that it was presented in an appropriate way. Nowadays an increasing number of researchers believe precisely the opposite: that there exists a multitude of intelligences, quite independent of each other; that each intelligence has its own strengths and constraints; that the mind is far from unencumbered at birth; and that it is unexpectedly difficult to teach things that . . . challenge the natural lines of force within an intelligence and its matching domains.[7]

By now, many of Gardner's conclusions should sound familiar. For instance, he points out that "the mind is far from unencumbered at birth" and it is not a "blank slate [that] could be trained to learn anything"; rather, each child is born with a bent toward a specific type of intelligence. Second, "it is unexpectedly difficult to teach things that . . . challenge the natural lines of force within an intelligence and its matching domains." If we do not recognize, affirm, and honor a child's God-given intelligence, we make it difficult for the child to learn.

The seven types of intelligence are explained below. The first two have been typically valued in schools; the next three are usually associated with the arts; and the final two are what Howard Gardner called "personal intelligences."[8] Which intelligences do you identify with most strongly? As you think of your loved ones, can you determine the intelligences in which they excel?

*Linguistic intelligence* involves sensitivity to spoken and written language, the ability to learn languages, and the capacity to use language to accomplish certain goals. This intelligence includes the ability to effectively use language to express oneself rhetorically or poetically and to use language as a means to remember information. Writers, poets, lawyers, and public speakers are among those that Howard Gardner sees as having high linguistic intelligence.

*Logical-mathematical intelligence* consists of the capacity to analyze problems logically, carry out mathematical operations, and investigate issues scientifically. According to Howard Gardner, it entails the ability to detect patterns, reason deductively, and think logically. This intelligence is most often associated with scientific and mathematical thinking.

*Musical intelligence* involves skill in the performance, composition, and appreciation of musical patterns. It encompasses the capacity to recognize and compose musical pitches, tones, and rhythms. Musical intelligence includes sensitivity to tones, voice inflections, and body language cues, which results in the ability to read other people quite well.

*Bodily-kinesthetic intelligence* allows someone to use the whole body or parts of the body to solve problems. It is the capacity to use mental abilities to coordinate bodily movements. For example, many people think more clearly when they're walking. Gardner sees mental and physical activity as related. Those with bodily-kinesthetic intelligence might become surgeons, athletes, or craftspeople.

*Visual-spatial intelligence* enables people to visualize in their "mind's eye." They think in pictures and images, seeing shape, light, depth, and color as if an object were right in front of them. This intelligence is exhibited by painters, pilots, graphic artists, and architects.

*Interpersonal intelligence* is concerned with the capacity to understand the intentions, motivations, and desires of other people. It allows people to work effectively with others.

Educators, salespeople, political leaders, and counselors all rely on a well-developed interpersonal intelligence.

*Intrapersonal intelligence* entails the capacity to understand oneself; to appreciate one's feelings, fears, and motivations; and then to be able to use such information to regulate one's life. Psychologists, philosophers, and spiritual leaders have high intrapersonal intelligence.

You have intelligence in all seven areas in a unique combination that only you possess. Most people will have one or two dominant intelligences, and those strengths tend to define how individuals learn and function best.[9]

## LIFE COACHING

Assessments such as those described above will help you determine the talents, personality, virtues, and intelligences that God has designed you with. They may be the first step to determining your unique genius. I think understanding your strengths in each of these areas is so key that I provide the latest resources and links to free information at the website www.thelanguageofblessing.com. At the back of this book, I've also included a list of recommended reading that will give you a greater understanding of these various types of giftedness.

Yet I urge you not to stop there. It is critically important that you involve others in your self-discovery journey. If someone at your church or workplace is trained to do life coaching, seek him or her out. If that is not an option, find a professional life coach in your community. You deserve to have someone come alongside you to help you in this all-important journey of a lifetime.

Let me use the StrengthsFinder assessment to illustrate the value of a coach as you seek to determine God's gifts in your life. As a coach myself, I have noticed a typical reaction from those who take this survey but have not yet consulted with anyone on it. I call it the 3-1-1-2 formula because it's become so predictable.

When people first review their assessment results, typically they tell me something like this:

3 of the top identified strengths make complete sense
   to them
1 makes no sense to them at all
1 of them doesn't seem like a strength
2 strengths they thought they possessed did not even
   rank in their top five

This causes them to discount many of the results. For instance, many people—men in particular—who take StrengthsFinder and score high in Harmony reject that talent outright or insist that it's not a strength. When I ask them why, I generally discover it's because they assume this talent means they are wishy-washy or seek peace at any price. Once I explain that this talent actually refers to the skill of helping people with divergent views find common ground, they better understand its value.

In addition, taking the assessment without processing the results seems to "inoculate" people from thinking much more about their strengths ("been there, done that"). As a life coach, I can ask my clients insightful and clarifying questions that help draw out details about their top five strengths—specifically, the strength that mystifies them, the one they don't perceive as a strength, and the two they had expected to make their top five but didn't. I can testify that people thoroughly enjoy discovering and talking about their gifts, talents, intelligences, and character strengths. And people love to be affirmed, valued, and celebrated by those who love and care about them.

The one thing they love even more? Using their unique gift to bless others!

## APPLICATION ACTIVITY

How aware are you of your strengths in the areas of talent, character and virtues, personality, and the multiple intelligences? Many people have limited self-awareness in all of these areas. I am always amazed at how miserly some people are toward finding out more about themselves. Many people think it is fine to spend fifty to one hundred dollars to go out for dinner and a movie, yet they hesitate to spend a similar amount on a few assessments that will help them discover critical information about themselves.

1. Have you taken any of the assessments covered in this chapter? If so, underline the statements in the report that resonate with you as real and authentic.

2. What did you learn about yourself from the assessment(s)?

3. Have you shared the results with anyone? Why or why not?

4. What insights did you gain regarding how you are different from those you love?

5. Which assessment will you take next? When? Whom will you share the results with?

Be sure to stop by www.thelanguageofblessing.com to learn more about additional resources and to find out how you might connect with a coach who is right for you.

*Chapter 9*

# CALM WITHIN THE STORM: CULTIVATING A NONANXIOUS PRESENCE

My number one talent, according to the StrengthsFinder assessment, is Ideation. I love being exposed to new ideas and then turning them around in my head, trying to make connections and formulate even more ideas.

In fact, I've even spent time ideating about the talent of Ideation! I enjoy taking two or more seemingly unrelated ideas and finding correlations that no one else has seen before. As a result, I know I need the freedom to live in ambiguity for a while as I sort through all of an idea's interesting turns, variations, and possibilities.

I've also determined that, in order to thrive, I need to spend time with other out-of-the-box thinkers. To refine my ideas, I rely on feedback from people who are willing to serve as sounding boards so I can bounce my ideas off them.

I have come to appreciate and value these traits in myself—and yet because I've now received the blessing, I don't expect all my family, friends, and colleagues to spend as much time considering ideas as I do. There are few things I love more than sitting with people and listening to them describe their own passions and proclivities.

By now you know my love for horticulture, so it may not surprise you that my outlook on coaching others mirrors something I learned from my maternal grandmother when I was very young. She and my grandfather lived on a farm in Iowa about two hours from where my parents, my siblings, and I lived.

From the time I was three years old, I loved staying on the farm. I was amazed that you could put plain little seeds in the dirt and get flowers of every imaginable color and vegetables of every flavor!

When I was about six, my grandmother spread out a variety of seeds in front of me. As I carefully examined them, Grandma explained that the flat, oval, dark ones would produce watermelons and the flat, oval, white ones would turn into pumpkins. From the wrinkled, round, green ones, she'd get peas; from the oval, speckled ones, green beans; from the small, round, reddish-brown ones, radishes; and from the fine, thin ones, carrots.

As I held a flat, dark one, I asked, "So in this little seed are all the vines and the leaves and the great big watermelons—that's all in this little seed?"

My grandmother replied, "Yes, Joey, all you need to do is to put the watermelon seed in the soil where the sun will shine. When you add water, all the vines and leaves and watermelons will come out of that little seed you have in your hand."

With eyes wide, my mouth sagged open in awe as I tried to ponder the significance of what Grandma had just told me.

As I grew a bit older, my grandmother explained that each plant required different amounts of sunlight, moisture, fertilizer, soil type, and spacing. "Those big watermelons and cantaloupes you love so much," she said, "they like sandy, rich, loamy soil. Because they need good drainage, we make a big mound when we plant them. Both plants are also heavy feeders, so we give them lots of fertilizer. Oh, and they need lots of sun, lots of water, and plenty of room to grow."

"What about carrots?" I asked. "How do you grow those?"

My grandmother replied, "Carrots also like sandy, loamy soil, but not too much fertilizer or they get all hairy! But we can put lots of carrots in a small space."

Then I asked, "What about peas? I love to eat them right out of the pods as we pick them."

"Peas like cooler weather so we plant them in early spring, and they need support for their vines." Each plant, I learned, thrives in its own optimal growing environment.

People are a lot like those seeds. Wonderful, valuable attributes are inside each person, and they're just waiting to be nurtured and developed. Just as plants require varying amounts of sunlight, water, and nutrients to thrive, so people all have certain needs in common—safety and nourishment, as well as our physical, emotional, and spiritual well-being— yet what we require to meet those needs varies from person to person.

Like me, some people are energized when they're exposed to new ideas; others find that tedious but come alive when they walk into a room full of people they've never met. Some people feel most comfortable and productive in a consistently predictable workplace; others find such an environment boring and draining. When things do not go as planned, some people experience extreme stress; other people are energized and highly motivated by surprises. Some want great variety in their daily work; others prefer to stick with the tried and true. Some people thrive in the spotlight, while others would rather remain behind the scenes. Some need frequent interaction with other people, while others are energized by long stretches of alone time.

*People who develop their unique gifts appear to go through dramatic changes, but in reality, they are just becoming more of what they actually are.*

✦ ✦ ✦

The combination of each person's needs is ultimately unique to that person, just as his or her talents, gifts, character, and intelligences are. If the unique needs are sufficiently satisfied, then the person thrives and functions as God intended. If someone's unique needs are not met, then that person struggles and does not function according to his or her God-given design.

Like seeds that transition from sprouts to fully mature, fruit-bearing plants, people who develop their unique gifts appear to go through dramatic changes, but in reality, they are just becoming more of what they actually are. Ideally, as we grow and mature, we become more authentic expressions of who God created us to be.

## THE BENEFITS OF APPRECIATING YOUR UNIQUENESS

So what does this refresher course in horticulture have to do with the blessing? Aside from better understanding how you can fulfill your own potential, once you've been blessed and affirmed for your own unique genius, you're better able to nurture other people by being sensitive to their needs.

In 1984 Edwin Friedman, a family therapist and rabbi, released a landmark book called *Generation to Generation* in which he urges clergy to know themselves well enough that they can be truly present with those they are leading.

In his final book, *A Failure of Nerve*, which was published posthumously, Friedman says the most effective leader is "someone who has clarity about his or her own life goals, and, therefore, . . . is less likely to become lost in the anxious emotional processes swirling about." Furthermore, such a leader "can be separate while still remaining connected, and therefore can maintain a modifying, nonanxious, and sometimes challenging presence."[1]

In other words, once you and I have received the blessing,

we are free to pass that blessing on to our children, coworkers, friends, and others. We are able to celebrate their God-given talents, personality, and character traits rather than judging them for not being more like us. One way we do that is by encouraging them to explore their unique makeup in what Friedman terms our "nonanxious presence."

Becoming more self-aware doesn't mean we become more self-focused; instead, it frees us to notice and bless others without minimizing or projecting our gifts onto them. It equips us to distinguish between those factors that motivate us and those that motivate others.

The apostle Paul provides a word picture of what it looks like to live with such an outlook:

> *Don't think you are better than you really are. Be honest in your evaluation of yourselves, measuring yourselves by the faith God has given us. Just as our bodies have many parts and each part has a special function, so it is with Christ's body. We are many parts of one body, and we all belong to each other. In his grace, God has given us different gifts for doing certain things well.* (Romans 12:3-6)

## NONANXIOUS PRESENCE

Remember Nora, whose story I told in the last chapter? More than likely, Nora's crying episodes as a little girl made her dad uncomfortable, perhaps even embarrassed. As a result, his response was curt: "Stop it. There's no reason to cry." Rather than acknowledging Nora's tendency to feel deeply and empathize with others, he sought to soothe his own anxiety by shutting her down—which, of course, only generated more fear in his daughter.

Nora found freedom after taking the StrengthsFinder assessment and understanding that empathy was truly a gift; not only that, it was a gift that others greatly appreciated. Even before receiving the blessing in this way, Nora displayed empathy. Yet she did so in a guarded manner, never sure that this quality had value. Furthermore, she was constantly looking to others for validation since she didn't see the incredible worth God had given her. As a result, her own family and coworkers sometimes felt as if they, too, were not enough for Nora.

Once she received the blessing in her own life, Nora was finally free to affirm and bless others for the way God has made them. She is now able to live with a nonanxious presence. Simply put, that means because she is now comfortable in her own skin, she can interact with others in a calm, peaceful, nonjudgmental way. In such an environment, other people are able to relax in her presence as well. After all, she is not looking to them to meet her needs; she now has the validation, purpose, and significance she once craved. Any fear her family or coworkers have that they are not enough for Nora dissipates.

I often say we cannot give what we have not received. Until you receive the blessing yourself, it will be nearly impossible to affirm anyone else's gifts and talents. Why is that?

In chapter 5, which introduced the Cycle of False Identity, I explained why those caught in the cycle of minimization, projection, and judging operate out of fear. When people are focused on themselves, fear drives their reaction to others. The antidote? "Perfect love expels all fear" (1 John 4:18). While fear is fixated on the internal, love is always focused outward:

> *Love is patient, love is kind. It does not envy, it does not boast, it is not proud. It does not dishonor others, it is not self-seeking, it is not easily angered, it keeps no record of wrongs. Love does not delight in evil but rejoices with the truth. It always protects, always trusts, always hopes, always perseveres.* (1 Corinthians 13:4-7, NIV)

Researchers have discovered that fear actually shuts down parts of our brains. It keeps us from empathizing, from listening actively to others, and from responding thoughtfully and nonreactively. When we give or receive love, on the other hand, every part of the brain is able to flourish, and we are able to be totally present to others. That doesn't mean we will make people happy all the time; it does mean we can live with the peace that comes from knowing we are fulfilling God's will for our lives.

Jesus is our model for living with a nonanxious presence.

Just consider the first few chapters of the Gospel of Mark. Chapter 1 contains story after story of Jesus healing the sick, including Simon Peter's mother-in-law, and the demon possessed. Then, in verse 35, we read that before day-break after another busy day, Jesus headed out to an isolated place to pray to His heavenly Father.

Meanwhile, the disciples were interrupted early that morning by more sick people clamoring to see Jesus. Can't you imagine Simon Peter

> *When we give or receive love, every part of our brain is able to flourish, and we are able to be totally present to others.*
>
> ✦ ✦ ✦

and the other disciples anxiously looking all over town for Him? Perhaps they even thought, *How could Jesus slip out and leave us to deal with an unhappy mob of angry people?* When they finally found Him, they said, "Everyone is looking for you" (Mark 1:37).

Instead of panicking or merely giving in to the crowd's demands, Jesus calmly told His disciples, "We must go on to other towns as well, and I will preach to them, too. That is why I came" (verse 38). Jesus was free to follow His Father's will because He was motivated by love, not by fear that He would disappoint the people of Peter's hometown.

*Yes,* you might think, *but Jesus is fully God. How can I be that calm and cool when people have unrealistic expectations of me?*

For the answer, we need only look to the apostle Paul. After enduring much opposition and suffering, Paul writes to the Philippian church from a prison cell. Even though he has no idea when—or even if—he'll be released, he tells them,

> *Don't worry about anything; instead, pray about*
> *everything. Tell God what you need, and thank him*
> *for all he has done. Then you will experience God's*
> *peace, which exceeds anything we can understand. His*
> *peace will guard your hearts and minds as you live in*
> *Christ Jesus.* (Philippians 4:6-7)

That is the secret to remaining calm and at peace in any situation—we must stay attuned to the same still, small voice of God. He is the ultimate source of blessing in our lives.

Other than living with nonanxious presence, how do we speak the language of blessing? That's the question we'll take up in the next chapter.

**APPLICATION ACTIVITY**

I have discovered that the concept of nonanxious presence is a powerful coaching tool. I introduce it in my seminars and to all those I coach. People often find that learning to be aware when they become anxious and then discovering why they are feeling anxious can be very liberating for them. It has even helped them to be far more effective at work, at ministry, and at home. It is amazing what you can do when your brain is fully functional and self-aware!

Whenever you begin to feel anxious, ask yourself this simple question: *What am I afraid of?* Generally, the root cause is one of three main issues: a need for control; a need for safety and security; or a need for love, acceptance, or respect. For example, I noticed on a recent 1,200-mile road trip that I was frequently anxious while driving. At one point, I was driving on a four-lane highway directly behind a young lady talking away on her cell phone. She had passed me just a few minutes before; now she was driving ten miles per hour slower than I had been when she'd passed me.

My thoughts about this woman were definitely not words of blessing. I caught myself quickly and asked myself why I was anxious. Surprisingly, I realized I was not concerned about my safety, even though she was weaving like someone under the influence. No, what got me was that she had passed me and was now oblivious to the fact that she was delaying my progress. How dare she! I felt a loss of control in my situation, and I felt that she had disrespected me, which was silly. She did not know anything about me, other than that I was the person driving the car behind her.

I began to pray that God would bless her abundantly in every aspect of her life. As soon as I did, I was no longer anxious; instead, I was curious as to how long she would remain unaware of the effects of her behavior. A few minutes later she ended her call and instantly became conscious of her sluggish pace. She promptly sped up to at least twenty miles per hour over the speed limit. If I had not been aware of my anxiousness and prayed about it, my instinctive behavior would have been to gun my engine, scowl at her as I passed, and then pull into the lane closely in front of her—just so she would notice that I would not tolerate the indignity of her behavior. Now that would have been operating out of my Neanderthal brain!

1.  When did you last feel anxious when interacting with someone else?

2.  What were you afraid of?

# Chapter 10

# LEARNING A NEW LANGUAGE: PRACTICAL WAYS TO AFFIRM OTHERS

The blessing takes hold powerfully in community. That became crystal clear to me when I was leading a discipleship-training process I founded at my church a number of years ago.

I'll never forget my final session with the first group I led through the course. We had spent the previous six Wednesday nights doing classwork and then interacting with the members of our small groups.

Everyone had seemed fully engaged throughout the sessions, and I was certain that something significant, even transformational, would happen during our final session. I expected this evening to be the most high-energy and fun time so far. After all, this was the night everyone would share the dreams that God had created them to fulfill.

The class broke up into their small groups, but I quickly became alarmed as I looked around. Instead of high-fiving and laughing, I saw a room full of sober people, many in tears. Their response was so perplexing and unexpected that I just let them continue sharing until it was time to wrap up the meeting.

I could not imagine ending on this somber note. I wanted another chance for a more "upbeat" ending of our time together. So as the session ended, I announced we would meet one more time so we could each share with the whole class what we had identified as our calling. Everyone agreed to come back the following week.

I asked three participants to stay after and talk with me. My confusion must have been obvious because all three individuals were laughing as they came up to me.

One of them asked, "Joe, you have no idea what was happening tonight, do you?"

"Well," I said, "I was hoping you three would enlighten me."

A businessman I had known for some time spoke up first. He said, "Joe, as you know, I have been pretty successful in my business, but until tonight I never felt a sense of significance. For the very first time in my life, I understand who God has uniquely created me to be."

When the other two participants affirmed that they'd had a similar experience, I breathed a sigh of relief.

I thought back to the first evening we had met. While everyone had been pleasant from the start, I remembered that they had seemed self-conscious, even a little fearful.

What if they had no gifts or identifiable calling? Their fear had made them inwardly focused and a bit guarded. Over the following weeks, I had watched them open up a bit more as they began discovering the abundance of talents and gifts among them.

Thinking back to the snatches of conversations I'd heard as I wandered through the room that night, I realized I'd heard many participants saying to one another, "Tell me about your dream," or, "Tell me about how God is calling you to use your gifts and talents." They were completely outwardly focused—a 180-degree change from that first night. They were no longer comparing themselves to one another; instead, they sincerely wanted to learn about the other people in their small groups and find ways to help them fulfill their callings. As their trust and love for one another grew, they began to embrace a mutual interdependency. They had become experts at speaking the language of blessing in an environment of nonanxious presence.

God's heart, the Father's heart, is to bless His workmanship, to love His workmanship, to celebrate His workmanship in each one of us. Before He created the world, He was thinking of us, calling out to us, inviting us to be a part of His eternal purposes. He has chosen us to be vehicles of His blessing to one another. As parents, as spouses, as leaders, and as friends, we are to bless one another. As Christians, God gives us the privilege of affirming and motivating one another "to acts of love and good works" (Hebrews 10:24). We are blessed to be a blessing.

The reality, however, is that most churches are not places where members regularly bless one another. Most families do not excel at blessing one another either. People often think good thoughts of others, but they seldom express those thoughts in words. What is lacking is a robust language to affirm and bless one another.

*People often think good thoughts of others, but they seldom express those thoughts in words.*

✦ ✦ ✦

The ability to recognize and affirm gifts, talents, and character in others is an essential part of giving the blessing to one another. How exactly do we do that?

## TEN KEYS FOR OBSERVING GIFTS AND TALENTS

One of my favorite activities is watching my grandchildren play because it reveals so much about them. I remember the first time I saw my grandson Connor displaying one of his gifts. As his dad chatted with us, three-year-old Connor quickly became bored and tired of sitting. After walking around the room and peering inquisitively at the items in the room, he asked if he could go down to our home's lower level to find a toy to play with.

"Of course," I said, and down he went. My wife, son, and I continued to chat for well over an hour before we all realized that Connor had not come back upstairs.

I went down to check on him and found Connor sitting on the floor creating his version of a metropolis. After raising five sons, we had several storage boxes of LEGO pieces, and he had discovered this treasure trove. By now he had attached hundreds of the pieces to a large gray sheet of plastic. He had made towering skyscrapers and buildings of all shapes and sizes, while leaving space for streets and sidewalks.

I was amazed by the complexity of this model city my three-year-old grandson had made. I asked my son to come down and look. He was almost as shocked as I was by the detail Connor had incorporated into his city. He told me that, even though Connor had a set of wooden blocks, he had never played with LEGOs before.

Since that time, whenever Connor visits us, he enthusiastically hugs us, chats briefly, and then heads for the LEGO boxes. Connor loves creating things with space and dimension.

I didn't give Connor any sort of assessment. I just watched him. My grandson's happy, focused behavior was typical of someone exercising a natural talent. I have found that there are ten specific characteristics that people display whenever they are operating in one of their gifts or strengths. As you seek to uncover gifts and talents—whether in yourself or in the people you care about—keep these ten keys in mind.

### Key #1: It is enjoyable

God has built into us the intrinsic motivator of enjoyment so that whenever we are using one of our talents, we feel pleasure. Now, not everything that is fun and pleasant is an indicator of talent, but it is deeply enjoyable to operate in our talents. Obviously Connor loves creating three-dimensional block structures, which is a clear indication of his spatial intelligence.

### Key #2: Learning comes naturally

Connor was never given any instructions in building with LEGOs. He naturally understood how the pieces went together and how they could be connected to the LEGO board.

Likewise, in our individual areas of talent, we seem to be prewired with certain instructions; it is almost as if we already know what we need to know. This may seem all the more remarkable when we discover that most other individuals actually struggle to learn what we grasp as second nature.

### Key #3: No awareness of time

Even though Connor, like many boys, has a very high energy level and often finds it difficult to sit still, he will work quietly for more than three hours at a time creating complex model cities from LEGO pieces.

*In our individual areas of talent, we seem to be prewired with certain instructions; it is almost as if we already know what we need to know.*

✦ ✦ ✦

This is an example of what bestselling author Mihaly Csikszentmihalyi refers to as "flow"—those instances when our "sense of time becomes distorted"[1] because we are so engaged with a certain activity. As the old saying goes, "Time flies when you're having fun." It does, doesn't it?

### Key #4: Satisfaction

When Connor finishes one of his LEGO masterpieces, I can see a glimmer of gratification in his eyes. Likewise, one sign of a person's talent is his or her obvious sense of accomplishment in that activity.

### Key #5: Increased energy

I am very high in a StrengthsFinder talent called Input. People with this talent are intensely curious, and most of us love to read. My dear wife calls me a "voracious" reader. While many people read before bedtime to help them fall asleep, reading has the opposite effect on me. If I start to read a book and the subject matter is of interest to me, I become so energized that I will not be able to fall asleep for hours.

The same is true whenever we function in one of our talents—as we do, we'll find ourselves feeling invigorated. Of course, the opposite is also true: when we try to function in areas where we are not talented, we are likely to find them difficult and draining. So many people come home from work completely exhausted because they are trying to operate outside their talents, and they pay a high price for attempting to do so.

### Key #6: Increased focus

When we are using one of our talents, we naturally focus our energy and attention on what we are doing. It is as if we are drawn into the activity. It is almost effortless.

### Key #7: No self-consciousness

When we operate within our talents, our focus, energy, and sheer enjoyment cause us to give ourselves completely over to the activity, as well as those we may be doing it with. We become outwardly focused, which is a great experience.

When we try operating outside of our talents, on the other hand, we are very self-conscious. We are so aware that we are not doing something well—and sense that others also notice our failure to excel.

### Key #8: In the zone

Top performers—whether on the athletic field, onstage, in the laboratory, or in the classroom—refer to the feeling when these first seven characteristics come together as being "in the zone." They describe this as an exhilarating experience, one in which they feel intensely alive and deeply joyful. We can each experience being in the zone as we align our gifting and talents with our purpose and calling.

### Key #9: A feeling of authenticity

When using one of their talents, a person will think, *This is who I am. This feels "real" for me. I am being myself when I can use these talents and strengths in this way.*

### Key #10: Multiple settings

Whether at home, the workplace, school, or church—whether working, relaxing, or even while on vacation—people love using their talents and strengths anywhere.

# BECOMING A MASTER AT BLESSING

While these ten keys are useful whether you are seeking to uncover gifts in yourself or in other people, I have discovered that our mind-set is extremely important when trying to discern the unique genius in someone else. To speak the language of blessing in another person's life, you must practice these three habits:

## 1. Demonstrate Intentionality and Commitment

Becoming a person of blessing costs something. Words of blessing that will transform another person's life require an investment of time and effort. For our words to take root, those we seek to bless must view our words of affirmation as authentic and offered without any agenda other than their good.

The language of blessing might sound like this:

> *Words of blessing that will transform another person's life require an investment of time and effort.*
>
> ✦ ✦ ✦

- "Luciana, you are such a kind and caring person. You can sense and express what others feel in such a special way. What a beautiful gift."
- "Mike, you ask such great questions. It really shows how deeply you think about things before you ask. That really helps us all. Thank you."
- "Tom, when you invite people over for dinner, even if there are more than a dozen guests, you remember how each of us prefers our salad, how we like our

steaks cooked, and even how we like our after-dinner coffee. You are amazing!"

- "Jennifer, I am so proud of how you reached out to that girl in your class when she was being ignored by the other girls. That was so considerate and caring of you."

- "Isaiah, you really know how to explain complex ideas in a way that we can all understand. You have such a gift."

We so often think thoughts like these, but sadly, most are not verbalized in a meaningful way. Let's start saying them, even if people minimize their gifts in their response to our words or even if they act a little embarrassed—say such things anyway. Most people have not had a chance to learn how to receive sincere words of affirmation and blessing. The more opportunities you provide, the better they will become at it.

Observing people's behavior and trying to understand why they do what they do has been a lifelong passion for me. I realize my passion is partially a result of my gifts, talents, and character. Yet even with God-given inclinations that compel me to try to better understand others, I must be deliberate about paying attention.

Listening intentionally to another person comes easier to those with a nonanxious presence because they are able to focus on others. They are positioned to listen well, be in the moment, and respond thoughtfully. Let's take a closer look at each of these communication skills:

- *Active listening:* We listen with respect and focused interest so we can better know and understand another person. We do so with the realization that this person is the world's expert on his or her unique design.
- *Responsiveness to the present moment:* We pay special attention to voice tone and inflections, facial expressions, and body language as the other person communicates.
- *Ability to respond in a thoughtful, nonreactive way:* We understand that the language of blessing is about the other person, not us. We ask insightful and clarifying questions to show our growing understanding and our genuine interest in this person.

## 2. Become a Student of the Other Person

If you want to be a master gardener, you have to learn the unique requirements of all the plants you wish to grow. Becoming a "master" of blessing requires that you become a student of those you love and desire to bless.

Novak Djokovic, who was rated the world's top tennis player at the beginning of 2012, owes his career to another tennis legend: Jelena Gencic, an outstanding Yugoslav tennis and handball player who later made a name for herself as a coach for Monica Seles and other top players.

At age four, Novak began playing tennis on the courts across the parking lot from the restaurant his parents ran. Two years later, he spent an entire morning watching Gencic lead a tennis camp on those same courts. Afterward, she invited him to attend the clinic the following day, which he did.

After watching him a second day, Gencic called his parents and told them, "You have a golden child." From that point on, his parents sacrificed a great deal to ensure Novak had all the training and equipment he needed—even as they watched war erupt between the Bosnians and the Serbs following the breakup of Yugoslavia.[2] While you may not discover the world's next top-seeded tennis player, you can call out what is "golden" in your children, your spouse, your neighbor, or your employee.

If you are serious about better understanding someone, the assessments we studied in the previous chapter provide what I call "relational shorthand." They give you a quick snapshot of someone's gifts and create a starting point for the two of you to talk about that person's strengths, inborn traits, and motivators.

### 3. Look for a Person's Internal Motivators

Too often we assume people are energized to act by the promise of recognition or some tangible reward or, on the negative side, from fear of losing their jobs or embarrassing themselves—in other words, we assume people respond most strongly to extrinsic motivators.

A growing body of research, however, points to a much different reality. Consistently, great performers display intense intrinsic motivation. Their desire for excellence compels them to stretch past their comfort zone and constantly try to improve. They realize that no discomfort means no growth.

What gives individuals this kind of drive and determination? I believe that each of our gifts and talents has powerful intrinsic motivators. All people have within themselves a potential "fire in the belly"—one or more internal drivers that enable them to develop the gift within, let their light shine, achieve great things, and contribute their unique genius to the world.

Do you remember the story of Susan from chapter 3? Her experience so beautifully illustrates this concept. When she first came to New Life, she was physically, emotionally, and spiritually exhausted and beat-up. She was in despair and had all but given up on life. Those close to her had used her gifts and talents—her kindness, her compassion, and her desire to serve others—against her. They had received these wonderful attributes from her without offering any gratitude or acknowledgment of their value in return.

Because she did not realize the great value of her unique gifts and talents, Susan never set any boundaries in her life. As a result, her husband and her children constantly took from her until she had nothing left to give.

When she was a little girl, Susan had had a vibrant dream and calling deep inside her to help others. By the time she arrived at New Life, however, she'd become enmeshed in the Cycle of False Identity. Her passion had been beaten down until it was almost invisible. Susan herself was no longer aware it even existed. But once she shared her journey to despair without any sugarcoating, her New Life small group began to affirm her for her courage to be so open and transparent. Susan had been prepared for more rejection; instead, she began to feel truly accepted, even valued for who she was. In the newfound safety of her group, Susan's gifts and talents began to emerge as she encouraged and affirmed others when they told their own stories. The members of the group then affirmed her for her kindness, forgiving spirit, insights, and ability to quickly recognize the value in other people. They were modeling the Cycle of Authentic Identity, which is illustrated below.

Many people have not had their gifts and talents recog-

## Cycle of Authentic Identity

6. Offering your gift

1. Self-awareness

God's perfect love
Nonanxious presence
Identity based on unique
purpose/serving others
Abundance mentality
Outward focus

2. Gratitude

5. Love

3. Humility

4. Authenticity

nized and affirmed. What should be a raging fire within is only a smoldering ember, barely noticeable even to the individual. This ember needs to be coaxed back to life. Identifying smoldering embers and fanning them into flames is one of my great passions in life.

**APPLICATION ACTIVITY**

The ten keys (see pages 155–158) have been invaluable to me as I seek to discover my grandchildren's gifts and talents. They have been useful in other contexts as well. For instance, a church in Keller, Texas, has begun using these ten keys to help identify the strengths and gifts of children and young adults with special needs. For various reasons, many of these individuals are not able to take the assessments I have described in this book. I love the fact that this church community has taken the initiative to use this tool to bless these very special members of their congregation.

1. Take some time to consider during which activities you've seen these ten characteristics in your own life. Can you identify and describe one or more things you do that involve all ten?

2. How might you use these ten keys to bless people in your life?

*Chapter 11*

# NOT FOR PARENTS ONLY: EVERY CHILD IS AN OUTLIER

God's intention is that parents affirm His blessing in their children. For that reason, I want to direct this chapter to parents, who have the privilege of being involved in their kids' development from the beginning. All the principles I laid out in the last two chapters apply to everyone; now I want to turn my attention to two final elements of speaking the language of blessing that can best be done by parents.

If you don't have children living at home, I encourage you to consider the roles pruning and practice might play in the development of your own gifts and talents—or in the lives of those you supervise or mentor.

## PRUNING: REDUCING OPTION OVERLOAD

As you know, babies don't come with directions or a mission statement. Yet even before we meet our children for the first time, God has blessed them with gifts that begin to emerge quite early. Parents who are observant and willing can begin leading their children through a process of discovery, dreaming, and designing, all of which ultimately lead them to their destiny.

The foundation of discovery in childhood is providing a rich variety of activities and opportunities; observing the children while utilizing the ten keys from the previous chapter; and then asking clarifying questions and offering lots of encouragement. What activities and ways of thinking and relating to others come most naturally to them and make them come alive? Where is their potential?

Once people begin to understand the almost limitless possibilities that could be achieved through their gifts and talents, it is not uncommon for them to feel overwhelmed. This is especially true of young people who want to "keep all options on the table." Dreaming—or beginning to map out their personal vision of what they can uniquely contribute to the world—is a way for kids to begin deciding what areas to zero in on. Power comes from the focused development and use of these gifts. This vital focus develops through a process the Bible refers to as pruning.

*Power comes from the focused development and use of gifts—a process the Bible refers to as pruning.*

✦ ✦ ✦

When I was much younger, my wife and I moved into a home with a large backyard, and I decided to plant a Concord grapevine along the fence. One of my fondest childhood memories is going to the farmers market in October with my paternal grandmother and buying a basket of freshly picked Concord grapes. These baskets were at least fourteen inches long, eight inches wide, and six inches deep, with a handle in the middle. The baskets would hold several pounds of this culinary treasure. Each grape was about the size of a small marble and such a deep blue that it appeared almost black.

Once I'd grabbed a stem, I would put the first grape in my mouth and squeeze, which caused the tough grape skin to burst and release the most delicious part—fresh Concord grape juice. After savoring the juice, I would squeeze out the fleshy part, carefully chewing while avoiding the rather bitter-tasting seeds. Then I would repeat the steps, again and again. Eating these grapes was a slow and deliberate process but worth the effort.

Later, as a young father in a new home, I wanted my wife and sons to experience what I had so enjoyed as a young boy. The first year my new Concord grapevine grew only slightly, but it looked healthy. In the second year, the vine began to take off and grew ten canes. I'd read that I should cut the vine back to two primary canes during autumn. I did prune it back, though it seemed a bit extreme. Then came year three, when my Concord grapevine really took hold and grew like crazy! There must have been sixty or more new branches and canes. The following year, I was sure, would be the year of the harvest.

At the end of year three, I knew I was to cut back to

four primary canes, so I began to prune again. In no time I had cut enough branches to make a good-size grapevine wreath. I kept pruning until there were about ten large canes remaining. By then, I felt as if I had butchered the vine enough and stopped.

The following spring, my grapevine budded with even more vigor than before. Before long it was about thirty feet wide. The ten canes I had left the previous fall exploded with growth and soon held hundreds of clumps of grapes. Wow! I could picture my boys setting up a little grape stand in the fall and introducing the whole neighborhood to this very special fall treat.

As spring turned to summer I noticed that the grapes were not getting very big, but I was sure they would really plump up with a few more months of growing time. When summer began to turn to fall, my grapes were just starting to color up, but they still seemed small. Finally in mid-October they turned that beautiful midnight dark blue. Unfortunately, they were still tiny; in fact, it looked as though I would be harvesting a bumper crop of purple peas!

*Well sure, they are small,* I thought, *but the large number of grapes will surely make up for their small size.* Then I tried my first grape. When I squeezed the grape, instead of succulent Concord grape juice, out popped three large seeds. There was no juice and virtually no pulp, just seeds—bitter, full-size Concord grape seeds!

As I stood there, deeply disappointed, I felt the Spirit speak to me: *Joe, you are so very much like your grapevine. You have so much potential in so many ways, but unless you allow the Father to prune you—and your potential—you will never bear the fruit He created and called you to bear.*

I learned three things about being pruned: (1) it can be a painful and unpleasant experience, (2) it is a necessary and ongoing process, and (3) it produces new focus and energy for growth and fruitfulness. As I thought about the pruning in my own life, I realized that the Father would not prune me for fruitful service until I invited Him to do so and surrendered every branch—all my potential—to Him.

*Pruning produces new focus and energy for growth and fruitfulness.*

✦ ✦ ✦

As parents and mentors, we can assist in God's pruning by helping those we care about discover their unique God-given design early in life. Just as my grapevines could not support too many canes, our kids will not have the time or energy to pursue every option in life. Our role is to help them determine which "canes" have the most potential. We can help them align their gifts, talents, and intelligences with the desire in their hearts to make a meaningful difference, to contribute what they have uniquely received for the benefit of others. In other words, we can encourage them to concentrate on those areas in which they show particular natural ability and passion.

Once one or more talents have been discovered through pruning, the next part of the process is design—helping our kids determine the first steps to experiment with using their gifts and abilities. As they begin developing certain strengths, we can be there supporting and encouraging them. As anyone who has ever prepared for a musical recital or team tryouts knows, that requires practice.

## PRACTICE: OVERCOMING INERTIA

There have been some significant discoveries about why pruning that leads to focused effort is so important and why it is becoming even clearer that we were not created to be jacks-of-all-trades and masters of none.

In his book *Outliers*, Malcolm Gladwell provides valuable insight into how the Tiger Woodses, the Wayne Gretzkys, the Michael Jordans, and the Bill Gateses of the world develop their world-class talents. When individuals find something they love to do, something they have a real talent for and can practice deliberately until they reach the ten-thousand-hour mark, something almost magical happens. They leap to a new level of proficiency; they become world-class masters—outliers—set apart from the rest of us mere mortals. Gladwell cites this conclusion from Daniel Levitin, a prominent neurologist:

> "The emerging picture from such studies is that ten thousand hours of practice is required to achieve the level of mastery associated with being a world-class expert—in anything," writes the neurologist Daniel Levitin. "In study after study, of composers, basketball players, fiction writers, ice skaters, concert

pianists, chess players, master criminals, and what have you, this number comes up again and again. . . . [N]o one has yet found a case in which true world-class expertise was accomplished in less time. It seems that it takes the brain this long to assimilate all that it needs to know to achieve true mastery."[1]

Ten thousand hours seems like a lot of time to spend developing an area of talent. Is it even possible for the average kid? Picture a child who discovers something she is truly talented in and loves to do at ten years of age. That child then invests an average of 2.7 hours a day to practicing and developing this talent. Factoring in time off during holidays, she will hit the ten-thousand-hour mark by the time she reaches twenty-one!

Now, notice that the ten-thousand-hour phenomenon applies to developing *world-class* expertise. I'm not suggesting that every parent's goal should be to have their kids rack up thousands of hours practicing a certain activity. However, what I am saying is that expertise comes after consistent practice, and that is likely to happen only when kids are doing what they like and are good at. As Stephen J. Dubner and Steven D. Levitt, authors of the bestseller *Freakonomics*, point out: "When it comes to choosing a life path, you should do what you love—because if you don't love it, you are unlikely to work hard enough to get very good."[2]

Also keep in mind that children will spontaneously utilize aspects of their talent in everyday life. If they have gifts in communication, for example, they are likely to be drawn to opportunities for public speaking, acting in a community play, or writing for their school paper. In other words, some of those ten thousand hours will just happen naturally!

*Expertise comes after consistent practice, and that is likely to happen only when kids are doing what they like and are good at.*

✦ ✦ ✦

Gladwell refers to the home where parents encourage and support their children's passions as having an atmosphere of "concerted cultivation." These parents actively seek opportunities for their children to excel—whether in academics, sports, music, or social activities. They look for the talent, intrinsic motivation, and interest within their children for a particular activity, understanding that such an endeavor has the potential to grow into something significant for the child. These parents are students and advocates of their children. If they believe the children may not be getting the attention or opportunities they need from their teachers or coaches, they are not afraid to intervene for the children.

Please note that I am not advocating for helicopter parenting, which is exemplified by the stereotypically overbearing mom or dad trying to ensure that his or her child not only makes the team but then gets plenty of playing time in key positions. Often such parental interference is motivated by the adults' desire to live vicariously through their kids.

However, as I pointed out earlier, our educational system is not geared to working with what is special within each individual child. That's why parents need to be expert students of their own children and do what they can to provide their kids with the opportunities they need to fuel their passions and gifts.

The language of blessing is extremely powerful when spoken by parents—it affirms children's talents and ultimately points them to their destiny: the calling and purpose God has for them.

## HEARD IT THROUGH THE GRAPEVINE

If your parents did not speak the language of blessing, if they never seemed curious about your interests or engaged in your favorite activities, remember that God has already blessed you. Your task now is to go through the process of discovery, dreaming, and designing so you can live out your own destiny.

While the first harvest from my grapevine was not what I'd hoped for, the pleasure and joy I experienced while caring for those Concord grapes was just another confirmation of my love of horticulture. Over the years, I also uncovered my love for teaching and coaching people who, like me, long to discover and then live out God's purpose in their lives. Perhaps that is why I dream of one day opening an inn where people come together to discover the blessing God has put into each of their lives. In my mind's eye, this meeting place is surrounded by a lush lawn and gardens filled with colorful flowers, fruits, and vegetables.

In a sense, I am already beginning to live out this dream. My wife and I love to host guests in our home, and there are few things that bring me greater pleasure than whipping up a meal for all of us using some of the produce from our garden.

The point is this: If you have children in your life, please don't miss the incredible opportunity you have to help them uncover God's blessing in their lives. If you are an adult whose parents overlooked the blessing in you, know that you have been blessed by God as well. It's not too late to embark on your own journey of discovery, dreaming, and designing, which will ultimately lead you to your destiny.

## APPLICATION ACTIVITY

In the Western world, most of us do not suffer from too few options but rather far too many. This often causes a form of option overload. Research has shown that if you have two or three goals you hope to achieve in a realistic period of time, odds are you will accomplish all of them. If you set between four and ten goals, odds are you will accomplish one. If you have more than ten goals, the odds are that you will accomplish none of them by your deadline.

Most people have a large number of wants, desires, and

goals bouncing around in their heads, but they never write them down and prioritize them. They rather haphazardly or even compulsively do the quick and easy ones, without any sense of the cost to their other goals and desires. In other words, they do a poor job of "pruning" in their lives.

As part of my life coaching program, I introduce each person I coach to a system of prioritizing, which is designed to help them prune for greater productivity in their own lives. I ask them to make eight individual lists of the key areas of their lives: Family, Career, Finances, Spiritual Life, Living Environment, Personal Growth, Health and Fitness, and Social Life. On each list I ask them to write down everything they have ever wanted, desired, or dreamed about in each of these areas. I then take them through a process of prioritizing all eight areas. It is so enlightening to hear individuals use their core values to define their top priorities in each area of life.

Once they have established their number one priority in each of the eight areas, I ask them to rank all their number one priorities until they can identify two or three top priorities in their lives. We then strategize a process to realize each goal through the use of their unique set of talents, gifts, intelligences, experiences, and education. Once one goal is achieved, they can begin working on the next highest priority, always keeping their focus on just two or three top goals.

Go to www.thelanguageofblessing.com, where I provide tools you can use to go through this process in more detail. The resources there are free.

1.  Take some time to consider your top priorities in all eight
    key areas listed on page 177.

2.  What are your two or three top priorities overall?

3.  How could you translate those priorities into goals
    to accomplish this year?

# Chapter 12

# SPEAKING THE LANGUAGE: AN ACCENT ON GRATITUDE

"Tonight, for the very first time in my life, I experienced a profound sense of gratitude for who God has uniquely created me to be. I see now that I was created with a special combination of gifts and talents . . . for a purpose, a special purpose."

The man standing before me would have been considered successful by any outward measure. In fact, I introduced him to you at the beginning of chapter 10—he is one of the three people who stayed to talk with me after we finished a discipleship-training process.

Not only did this businessman come away from that group with a new sense of purpose, he displayed gratitude—a life-enriching characteristic that I consider the accent of the language of blessing.

"I understand that this is all grace," he told me. "I do not deserve this; I certainly did not earn it; I did not even ask for it. God, out of His love for me, has richly blessed me, and I am so thankful."

*Gratitude is a life-enriching characteristic that I consider the accent of the language of blessing.*

✦ ✦ ✦

As I've coached countless people through the gift-discovery process, I've come to realize that the language of blessing ultimately leads to an understanding that our Creator has freely given all of us abundant talents and gifts. We were each designed with purpose and meaning. Again and again, I have watched people be humbled by the reality that God's gifts and calling on their lives are completely unmerited. They are products of His endless grace.

People who have received the blessing in their own lives no longer need to compare themselves to others; instead, they sincerely want to learn more about other people and find ways to help them fulfill their calling. They want to speak the language of blessing.

## THE POWER OF GRATITUDE

This attitude of gratitude brings multiple benefits:

- Gratitude releases us from the bondage of comparison.

- Gratitude frees us from false humility.
- Gratitude enables us to let go of unfounded expectations. We can say, "no, thank you" without experiencing false guilt.
- Gratitude sets us free to love.
- Gratitude empowers us to be who God has called and created us to be.

Once you and I become truly grateful, we acknowledge that none of our gifts began with us. Everything began with Him. Our talents and strengths were given to us not primarily for our own benefit but for the benefit of others. When we understand that, we receive the incomparable great joy of offering all our gifts to others, knowing that we are unique and unrepeatable, that we exist for a reason.

It has been well over a decade since my epiphany about the importance of gratitude. Since then, I have focused mostly on working with adults in leadership positions, including many who have come to a crossroads in their lives—a crisis, if you will—and want to make significant changes.

Recently, though, I have been working with more young people, many of whom are just launching out on their own. I have discovered that most twentysomethings desperately want to know who they are and what their calling is. They want a connection, a sense of calling, and a purpose. I love that!

Despite this desire to find their destiny in life, many young adults are chafing under the unfounded expectations of others. They are just as prone to minimize as people in other age groups; but when you help them see how unique their talents, gifts, and character traits are, they light up with excitement! Once they have a sense of calling and destiny, they are quick to receive their gifts, talents, and character with great joy.

*When we have a sense of calling and destiny, we are quick to receive our gifts, talents, and character with great joy.*

✦ ✦ ✦

Whether we call it discipleship, mentoring, or coaching, speaking the language of blessing is worth the cost, time, and effort it requires to help others rediscover, develop, and live out their unique calling through their personality, gifts, talents, intelligences, and character. Please check out www.thelanguageofblessing.com for more free resources you can use as you continue learning to affirm others.

Jesus once said, "What you say flows from what is in your heart" (Luke 6:45). Live each day with intentionality, focus, and gratitude. Before you know it, you'll be speaking the language of blessing fluently.

## APPLICATION ACTIVITY

One of the most powerful and transformational disciplines I recommend to those I coach is to begin writing in a daily gratitude journal. As we finish this book, I encourage you to do the same.

It does not have to be anything fancy—a one-dollar notebook works just fine. Each evening, write down three things you are most grateful to God for from that day. It is amazing how quickly this little exercise will begin to change your attitude and outlook on life. By creating pathways of gratitude, you will intentionally rewire your marvelous brain. This will dramatically increase your times of nonanxious presence, which will significantly affect your ability to bless others in your life.

1.  What are the three things today that you are most grateful for?

2.  Now that you have come to the end of the book, what are one or two of the most valuable insights you will take away from *The Language of Blessing*? How do you hope these lessons affect the way you think and relate to others?

# Acknowledgments

Thanks to Jan Long Harris, publisher at Tyndale Momentum, bestselling author George Barna, and my literary agent, Esther Fedorkevich, all of whom had faith in a first-time author. Thanks to senior editor Kim Miller who was so patient, encouraging, and insightful throughout the editing process.

Thanks to my personal board of directors: Jon Reid, Bob Maybrey, and John Malek. All three men read my rough manuscript and offered valuable insights to improve this book. Other dear friends who gave equally valuable feedback include Elaine Burke, Lynette McCulloh, and Ken Hladek.

# Recommended Resources

I have selected the books that I believe will best help you understand your own unique design and the unique design of others.

## BLESSING OTHERS

Trent, John, and Gary Smalley. *The Blessing*. Nashville: Thomas Nelson, 1986.

## CHARACTER STRENGTHS AND VIRTUES

Peterson, Christopher, and Martin E. P. Seligman. *Character Strengths and Virtues*. New York: Oxford University Press, 2004.

## INDIVIDUALISM

Bellah, Robert N., Richard Madsen, William M. Sullivan, Ann Swidler, and Steven M. Tipton. *Habits of the Heart*. Berkeley: University of California Press, 2007.

## MULTIPLE INTELLIGENCES AND THE SCIENCE
## OF NEUROPLASTICITY

Leaf, Caroline. *The Gift in You.* Southlake, TX: Inprov, Ltd., 2009.

Leaf, Caroline. *Who Switched Off My Brain?* Southlake, TX: Inprov, Ltd., 2009.

## TALENT STRENGTHS

Rath, Tom, and Donald O. Clifton. *How Full Is Your Bucket?* New York: Gallup Press, 2004.

Winseman, Albert L., Donald O. Clifton, and Curt Liesveld. *Living Your Strengths.* New York: Gallup Press, 2003.

Rath, Tom, and Barry Conchie. *Strengths-Based Leadership.* New York: Gallup Press, 2008.

# *Endnotes*

## INTRODUCTION

1. Gary Smalley and John Trent, *The Blessing: Giving the Gift of Unconditional Love and Acceptance* (Nashville: Thomas Nelson, revised edition, 2011), 45.

## CHAPTER 1: The Blessing

1. "Memorable Quotes from *Hugo*," IMDB.com, http://www.imdb.com/title/tt0970179/quotes. Martin Scorsese (director). 2011. *Hugo*. Screenplay by John Logan based on the book *The Invention of Hugo Cabret* by Brian Selznick.
2. Drew McWeeny, "Review: Martin Scorsese's 'Hugo' Is a Rapturous Lesson in the Value of Art," *Motion Captured*, November 23, 2011, http://www.hitfix.com/blogs/motion-captured/posts/review-martin-scorseses-hugo-is-a-rapturous-lesson-in-the-value-of-art.

## CHAPTER 2: We Are His Workmanship

1. Edwin H. Friedman, *Generation to Generation: Family Process in Church and Synagogue* (New York: The Guilford Press, 1985).
2. Tate Taylor (director). 2011. *The Help*. Screenplay by Tate Taylor, based on the novel by Kathryn Stockett.

3. Caroline Leaf, *The Gift in You: Discovering New Life through Gifts Hidden in Your Mind* (Nashville: Thomas Nelson, 2009), 11.

4. Ibid., 35.

5. Gallup research shows that most people are far more focused on their weaknesses—what they are not—than on their strengths—what they are, unique masterpieces with God as the artist. How bad is it? After interviewing 1.7 million people in sixty-three countries, Gallup reported: "Globally, only 20 percent of employees working in the large organizations we surveyed feel that their strengths are in play every day. Most bizarre of all, the longer an employee stays with an organization and the higher he climbs the traditional career ladder, the less likely he is to strongly agree that he is playing to his strengths." Marcus Buckingham and Donald O. Clifton, *Now, Discover Your Strengths* (New York: Free Press, 2001), 6.

6. Tom Rath, *StrengthsFinder 2.0* (New York: Gallup Press, 2007), 7, italics in original.

7. Dan Rockwell, "When Restraint Takes You Further," *Leadership Freak* (blog), June 11, 2012, http://leadershipfreak.wordpress.com/2012/06/11/when-restraint-takes-you-further/.

## CHAPTER 4: The High Cost of Seeing Yourself as Average

1. Philip Roth, *American Pastoral* (New York: Houghton Mifflin, 1997), 35.

2. "Sydney J. Harris." BrainyQuote.com. Xplore Inc., 2012. http://www.brainyquote.com/quotes/authors/s/sydney-j-harris.html.

3. David L. Dotlich, "Adversity: What Makes a Leader the Most," January/February 2005, *Ivey Business Journal*, http://www.iveybusinessjournal.com/topics/leadership/adversity-what-makes-a-leader-the-most.

4. Tom Rath and Barry Conchie, *Strengths-Based Leadership* (New York: Gallup Press, 2008), 13.

5. George Reavis, *The Animal School* (Peterborough, NH: Crystal Springs Books, 1999), 12.

6. Caroline Leaf, *The Gift in You: Discovering New Life through Gifts Hidden in Your Mind* (Nashville: Thomas Nelson, 2009), 123.
7. Roth, *American Pastoral*, 23.

## CHAPTER 5: Losing Yourself in the Cycle of False Identity

1. *Merriam-Webster's*, 11th ed., s.v. "minimize."
2. *Merriam-Webster's*, 11th ed., s.v. "common sense."
3. *Wikipedia*, s.v. "common sense," last modified October 29, 2012, http://en.wikipedia.org/wiki/Common_sense.
4. Caroline Leaf, *The Gift in You: Discovering New Life through Gifts Hidden in Your Mind* (Nashville: Thomas Nelson, 2009), 123.
5. Ibid., 143.
6. Ibid., 146.

## CHAPTER 6: Me, Myself, and I: The Consequences of Focusing on Self

1. *Merriam-Webster's*, 11th ed., s.v. "self-esteem."
2. "In Schools, Self-esteem Boosting Is Losing Favor to Rigor, Finer-Tuned Praise," *Washington Post*, January 11, 2012, http://www.washingtonpost.com/local/education/in-schools-self -esteem-boosting-is-losing-favor-to-rigor-finer-tuned-praise /2012/01/11/gIQAXFnF1P_story_1.html.
3. Kristin D. Neff, "The Role of Self-Compassion in Development: A Healthier Way to Relate to Oneself," *Human Development* 52 (2009): 211–214.
4. Jean M. Twenge, *Generation Me* (New York: Free Press, 2006), 212.
5. Roy F. Baumeister, Joseph M. Boden, and Laura Smart, "Relations of Threatened Egotism to Violence and Aggression: The Dark Side of High Self-Esteem," *Psychological Review* 103, no. 1 (1996): 5–33.
6. Ibid., 29.

7. Robert N. Bellah, Richard Madsen, William M. Sullivan, Ann Swidler, and Steven M. Tipton, *Habits of the Heart: Individualism and Commitment in American Life* (Los Angeles: University of California Press: 1996), 334.

8. Note that "republican" does not refer to a political party but to a system of government in which the people hold the ultimate power through the representatives they elect.

9. A recent AARP survey found that self-reported chronic loneliness among forty-five- to sixty-five-year-olds has increased 75 percent in the last decade and now affects 35 percent of the entire baby boomer generation. It was the baby boomers who rejected wholesale the institutional structures and cultural patterns of their parents and enthusiastically embraced radical individualism, first in the form of expressive individualism and then in utilitarian individualism.

## CHAPTER 7: A Matter of Character: Why Your Parenting Style Matters

1. Sissela Bok, *Common Values* (Columbia, MO: University of Missouri Press, 1995, 2002), 10–11.

2. James C. Hunter, *The World's Most Powerful Leadership Principle* (New York: Crown Business, 2004), 29–30, italics in original.

3. Gwen Dewar, "Authoritarian Parenting: How Does It Affect the Kids?" ParentingScience.com, copyright 2010–2011, http://www.parentingscience.com/authoritarian-parenting.html.

4. Ibid.

5. Ibid.

## CHAPTER 8: Know Yourself: Becoming Self-aware

1. In 2002, Dr. Clifton was recognized as the "Father of Strengths-Based Psychology" and honored with an American Psychological Association Presidential Commendation. See http://www.gallup.com/corporate/1357/corporate-history.aspx#5.

2. Marcus Buckingham and Donald O. Clifton, *Now, Discover Your Strengths* (New York: Free Press, 2001), 48.

3. Ibid., 24.

4. Clifton Youth StrengthsExplorer, a talent-identifying assessment for children ten to fourteen years of age, is available for purchase online at https://www.strengths-explorer.com/. StrengthsExplorer differs from the Clifton StrengthsFinder in that it has ten themes of talent and children receive their top three talent themes.

5. In his paper, Anderson went on to describe the genius he saw in each of the thirty-four themes of talent. See "The Genius and Beauty Found within the Clifton StrengthsFinder Themes of Talent," http://www.apu.edu/strengthsacademy/pdfs/genius _beauty_found_within.pdf.

6. To learn more about Values in Action and the VIA Inventory of Strengths, see http://www.viacharacter.org.

7. Howard Gardner, *Frames of Mind: The Theory of Multiple Intelligences* (New York: Basic Books, 1993), xxiii.

8. Ibid., chapter 10.

9. To learn more about the seven intelligences, you can find the assessment in Dr. Caroline Leaf's book *The Gift in You* (Nashville: Thomas Nelson, 2009), 100. Several educational websites also offer a free multiple-intelligence survey.

## CHAPTER 9: Calm within the Storm: Cultivating a Nonanxious Presence

1. Edwin H. Friedman, *A Failure of Nerve* (New York: Church Publishing Inc., 2007), 14.

## CHAPTER 10: Learning a New Language: Practical Ways to Affirm Others

1. Mihaly Csikszentmihalyi, *Flow: The Psychology of Optimal Experience* (New York: Harper & Row, 1990), 71.

2. Christopher Clarey, "Behind Serbia's Rise in Tennis, a Star and His Family," *New York Times*, December 1, 2010, http://www .nytimes.com/2010/12/02/sports/tennis/02iht-SRDCDJOKOVIC .html?pagewanted=all.

## CHAPTER 11: Not for Parents Only: Every Child Is an Outlier

1. Daniel Levitin, *This Is Your Brain on Music: The Science of a Human Obsession* (New York: Penguin, 2007), 193, quoted in Malcolm Gladwell, *Outliers* (New York: Little, Brown and Company, 2008), 40.

2. Stephen J. Dubner and Steven D. Levitt, "A Star Is Made," *New York Times Magazine*, May 7, 2006, http://www.nytimes.com/2006/05/07/magazine/07wwln_freak.html?_r=1&pagewanted=all.

# Online Discussion *guide*

Take *your* TYNDALE READING
EXPERIENCE *to the* NEXT LEVEL

---

A FREE discussion guide for this book
is available at bookclubhub.net, perfect
for sparking conversations in your book
group or for digging deeper into the text
on your own.

# www.bookclubhub.net

*You'll also find free discussion guides for
other Tyndale books, e-newsletters, e-mail
devotionals, virtual book tours, and more!*

Barna Books encourage and resource committed believers seeking lives of vibrant faith—and call the church to a new understanding of what it means to be the Church.

For more information, visit www.tyndale.com/barnabooks.

BARNA